Feeding the Ancestors

FEEDING THE ANCESTORS

Tlingit Carved Horn Spoons

Anne-Marie Victor-Howe

Foreword by Rosita Worl

Photographs by Hillel S. Burger

Rubie Watson, Series Editor

Peabody Museum Press, Harvard University

Editorial direction by Joan K. O'Donnell
Copy editing by Jane Kepp
Series cover and text design by Kristina Kachele
Volume design and composition by Mary Sweitzer
Color separations by Oceanic Graphic Printing
Printed and bound in China by Oceanic Graphic Printing

ISBN 978-0-87365-403-6

Library of Congress Cataloging-in-Publication Data:

Victor-Howe, Anne-Marie, 1950-
Feeding the ancestors : Tlingit carved horn spoons / Anne-Marie Victor-Howe ; foreword by Rosita Worl ; photographs by Hillel S. Burger.
p. cm. — (Peabody Museum collections series)
Includes bibliographical references.
ISBN 978-0-87365-403-6 (alk. paper)
1. Tlingit Indians—Implements. 2. Tlingit Indians—Implements—Pictorial works. 3. Tlingit Indians—Social life and customs. 4. Tlingit Indians—Social life and customs—Pictorial works. 5. Tlingit Indians—Rites and ceremonies. 6. Tlingit Indians—Rites and ceremonies—Pictorial works. 7. Spoons—Social aspects—Alaska. 8. Spoons—Social aspects—Alaska—Pictorial works. 9. Alaska—Social life and customs. 10. Alaska—Social life and customs—Pictorial works. I. Peabody Museum of Archaeology and Ethnology. II. Title.
E99.T6V53 2007
736'.6—dc22
                    2007004296

∞ The paper used in this publication meets the minimum requirements of the American National Standard for Information Sciences—Permanence of Paper for Printed Library Materials, ANSI Z39.48-1984.

Frontispiece: Prince of Wales Island, Tongass National Forest. The rugged, forested terrain and complex waterways are typical of Southeast Alaska. John Hyde, photographer.

Drawings by Jim Gilbert on pages v and 86 (sea monster), 6 (Eagle/Raven family crest), 43 (mountain goat), 47 (raven and sculpin), 74 (frog), and 90 (raven) are from the book *Learning by Designing: Pacific Northwest Coast Native Indian Art,* Volume 1 (Union Bay, British Columbia: Raven Publishing Inc., 1999), by Jim Gilbert and Karin Clark. They are reproduced here with the kind permission of Karin Clark and Raven Publishing Inc. © Raven Publishing Inc.

Drawings by Edward Malin on pages 45 (octopus), 51 and 62 (Strong Man and sea lion), 58 (sea lion), 76 (dragonfly), and 88 (whale) are from his book *Totem Poles of the Pacific Northwest Coast* (Portland, Oregon: Timber Press, 1986). They are published with the kind permission of Edward Malin © Edward Malin.

Front cover: *Tlingit Cosmos,* by Celeste Worl. Oil on canvas, 40 x 60 inches. © Celeste Worl 2002. Courtesy of the artist. Photograph by Wendy McEahern Photography.

Back cover: Tlingit carved horn spoons. Left to right, PM 69-30-10/1757, 9731, 1745, 1725. T5118.1. Photograph by Hillel S. Burger © the President and Fellows of Harvard College.

Contents

Illustrations

COLOR PLATES

Sacred Spoons for Spiritual Guests

Rosita Worl

I first met the author in the early 1980s on St. Lawrence Island in the Bering Strait between Alaska and Siberia, where we were both engaged in field research among the Siberian Yup'ik living in Alaska. I could not then guess that the next time our paths would cross would be in Southeast Alaska and that Dr. Anne-Marie Victor-Howe would be studying Tlingit ceremonial spoons that were once used by my ancestors.

I remember seeing plain horn spoons stacked in an empty coffee can on my clan grandfather's kitchen table in Klukwan, but rarely did I see carved ceremonial spoons. Like other traditional regalia and objects that did not find their way to museums or private collections, those that remained in the possession of the Tlingits were generally stored away and brought out only on ceremonial occasions. Our traditional potlatches had not been outlawed like those of our Canadian brothers and sisters. However, until the late 1960s, our ceremonies, or the *ḵoo.éex'*, were held hidden from the disapproving eyes of Westerners. Our parents had grown up during a period when religious and civil authorities discouraged them from practicing our ancient customs and using our *at.óow* or clan objects. They wanted to be good citizens

Tlingit Movement by Celeste Worl.
Oil on canvas, 48 x 36 inches.
© Celeste Worl 2002.
Courtesy of the artist.

and Christians, but fortunately for us, they did not abandon our ceremonies or our ancestors. They continued to hold the ceremonies in which the spirits of our ancestors were fed.

I had grown up, like other Tlingits, participating in ceremonies and using our clan regalia and objects. I had also seen our treasures in the small museum in Juneau and in Erna Gunther's *Art in the Life of the Northwest Coast Indians* (Portland Art Museum, 1966). But nothing had prepared me for the grandeur that I would see at the Smithsonian's National Museum of Natural History. In 1971, a group of us traveled to Washington, D.C., to participate in the Folk Art Festival. A kind soul invited us to look at our collections from Southeast Alaska. We stood in awe as drawer after drawer was opened for us, revealing treasures that we had never before seen or even imagined existed. Up to that point, I hadn't realized the uniqueness of our art or fully appreciated the greatness of our ancestors as artists. Neither had I realized the extent of the immense collections held by museums. We were overwhelmed with pride, but at the same time, we were overcome with a quiet sadness as we began to wonder about the historical events that led to museums holding these collections. Later I would attend school at Harvard University, and without any conception of the demands of mounting an exhibition, I naively decided that I would do an exhibit, which I titled *Tlingit Aaní, Enter the Tlingit World*. This allowed me to have an office in the Peabody Museum basement, where I lived amidst the collection for two years and saw many of the carved spoons featured in this publication.

Several years ago, Dr. Victor-Howe contacted me in my position as President of the Sealaska Heritage Institute (SHI), advising me that she was interested in conducting a study of the carved horn spoons in the Peabody Museum collection. SHI is a tribal organization whose mission is to promote the Tlingit, Haida, and Tsimshian cultures of Southeast Alaska. Our mission also includes the study of our cultures and history, and to that end, we had established a Visiting Scholars' office. Those who are accepted as Visiting Scholars are provided logistical support, including access to our traditional scholars and introductions to tribal members in our communities. In some instances, we are also able to provide modest financial support. Visiting Scholars are expected to agree to abide by the SHI Research Policy, which basically outlines the ethics of doing research in Southeast Alaska.

I was especially pleased to renew my acquaintance with Dr. Victor-Howe. It also provided me an opportunity to continue working with the Peabody Museum, with whom we had a partnership on another project. We provided Dr. Victor-Howe an office, introduced her to the cultural resource specialists working for SHI, and identified others whom she might wish to interview.

Dr. Victor-Howe's work differs from most other academic research projects in that she initiated it in consultation and in partnership with a Native tribe. Rather than objects of study, we became collaborators. Additionally, this study is unique among books on Northwest Coast art, in that for the first time we have a project devoted solely to a study of carved ceremonial spoons. Most publications have included at most one or two carved spoons, if any, and have focused primarily on the monumental art or other types of "exotic" objects of the Northwest Coast Indians. Instead of totem poles, masks, or shamanic paraphernalia, Victor-Howe has chosen to study twenty-six intricately carved ceremonial spoons that represent the finest ceremonial spoons created by the Southeast Alaska Indians.

The author notes the resemblance between the carved handles of the spoons and totem poles, both of which have images carved on top of one another. She also explores the meaning of the ceremonial spoons to cultural descendants of the artists who made them—a feature also rare among other Northwest Coast art publications, which generally focus on the art history or aesthetics of our material culture. After she identifies the images on the carved spoons, Victor-Howe recounts the oral traditions associated with the animals or other features that are depicted on them. These stories are well known among the Tlingit and Haida, but the author rightly concedes that we may never know the full meaning of the crest images depicted on the spoons. She adds another dimension not commonly found in publications featuring Northwest Coast art in her attempt to identify the clan or clans that might have owned these spoons through identifying the images featured on them.

Indigenous readers and others will appreciate Victor-Howe's insight into the cultural context of these ceremonial spoons. With the photographs of the sacred spoons and her writing, she enters the integrated natural and supernatural worlds of the Southeast Alaska Indians. The host clan desirous of honoring its ancestors is able to transfer food to them through their presentations to guest clan members.

When the sacred spoon enters the mouth of the ceremonial guest, the ancestors of the host clan receive the gift of food. Spiritual and social balance is achieved. Members of opposite moieties—Eagle and Raven clans—are united, and through the presentation of *at.óow* or clan objects from both the host and guest clans, Eagle and Raven spiritual guests meet and join with their living descendants.

Through her study of a seemingly modest and often ignored ceremonial object, Dr. Victor-Howe also may have pointed the way to understanding a common feature seen in the carved ceremonial spoons, rattles, and other objects—the protruding tongue. This image has puzzled anthropologists and Natives alike, and some have conjectured that the tongue serves as a source of strength. Perhaps the tongue provides a spiritual bridge between the human and spiritual worlds or for the spirits to connect with the living.

Anne-Marie Victor-Howe's work offers insight into an area rarely studied before. It also raises in my mind a host of other questions that should be considered in the context of what we know about the Tlingit conception of the interrelationships between the natural and the supernatural. Perhaps the answers to these questions can lead to a greater understanding of a very complex culture that created beautiful and powerful spoons to feed their spiritual guests.

ACKNOWLEDGMENTS

I feel both fortunate and grateful when I think of all of the help I have had in writing this book. I was fortunate to find generous people with great knowledge of this specialized topic, and I am grateful to those who came forward to assist me. Two people in particular offered grants and in-kind services that made the creation of this book possible: Rubie Watson, then William and Muriel Seabury Howells Director of the Peabody Museum of Archaeology and Ethnology at Harvard University, and Rosita Worl, president of the Sealaska Heritage Institute in Juneau, Alaska. Dr. Worl also kindly agreed to write the foreword to the book.

Working with these extraordinary spoons was a journey into uncharted territory, but expert guides came forward to pore over the photographs with me, a process that brought me great pleasure. Identifying the crests and the stories associated with the spoons would have been impossible without the help of David G. Katzeek, leader of the Shangukeidí clan and Tlingit tribal historian in Southeast Alaska. David also reviewed the manuscript at several stages of its development. His steady presence has been invaluable.

Harold Jacobs, a Yanyeidí and leading Tlingit scholar, told me much about Tlingit history and language that has never been published and helped me identify many crests. He reviewed the manuscript and was a constant source of support and advice while I was researching and writing the book.

Steve Henrikson, curator of the Alaska State Museum, also reviewed the manuscript and made many useful comments, as did Bill Holm, curator emeritus of Northwest Coast collections at the Burke Museum of Indian Art; Nathan P. Jackson, master carver; Sergei Kan, professor of anthropology and Native American studies at Dartmouth College; and Chuck Smythe, ethnography program manager for the National Park Service, Northeast Region, Boston. All these scholars and historians gave graciously of their time and knowledge.

Throughout this project, I was extremely fortunate to have had the advice of Tlingit and Haida scholars, elders, and writers, who have been generous in sharing their knowledge. I would like to recognize the contributions of the following Tlingit consultants, whose breadth of knowledge made the book possible and authoritative: Chris Burke, William Burkhart, Doug Chilton, Nora Marks Dauenhauer, Richard Dauenhauer, Sonny Grant, Joe Hotch, Marc Jacobs Jr., Leonard John, Anna Katzeek, Cecelia Kunz, Anita Lafferty, Jim Marks, Johnny Marks, Louis Minard, and Thomas Young. Also, by inviting me to the "last potlatch" and bringing me into their family, clan elder Matilda Gamble and her son, Andrew Gamble, clan leader of the Kaag-waantaan Wolf House in Sitka, gave me an invaluable opportunity to understand their tradition.

My Haida sources, Jan Burguess, Robin Field, Charles Natkong, Clarence Peel, and Warren Peel, also responded magnanimously with their time and knowledge. Vicky LeCornu graciously hosted me and facilitated my research during several field trips to Hydaburg, on Prince of Wales Island.

Other experts, including Peter Corey, former curator of the Sheldon Jackson Museum in Sitka, Alaska, and Willis Osbakken, also stepped forward to help identify the crests carved on the spoons. At the Sealaska Heritage Institute in Juneau, Bessie Cooley and Yarrow Vaara provided important information about the Tlingit language and traditional customs. At the Peabody Museum, Susan Haskell smoothly facilitated my access to the spoon collection, and T. Rose Holdcraft and Scott Fulton patiently answered many questions about the materials used in the spoons' manufacture.

Donna Dickerson, projects manager at the Peabody Museum Press, guided me expertly in the details of manuscript development. I also owe special thanks to the staff at the Tozzer Library, Harvard, for their patient assistance with my research, both online and off. At the Alaska State Library in Juneau, Gladi Kulp and Kay Shelton were consummate professionals, tracking down and answering many questions about the historic photographs I used in my research and as illustrations for the book. Bridget Smith and Helen Snively helped copyedit early versions of the manuscript, and Jane Kepp performed a masterful edit of the final manuscript. Mary Sweitzer created the beautiful layout of the text.

Dan Jones, Photo Archives Associate at the Peabody Museum, spent many hours taking excellent photographs of the spoons that were extremely important for my research and the project website. I am equally fortunate that Steve Burger, former staff photographer at the Peabody, agreed to take the superb photographs that illustrate this book. I am also grateful to Joel Bennett for his wonderful close-up shots of a Dall sheep and a mountain goat; to John Hyde for photographs of Alaska's landscape that capture the essence of the place; and to James Poulson, photographer for the *Daily Sitka Sentinel*, who kindly allowed me to use several photos of an important Tlingit potlatch held in 2004.

Several people very kindly gave permission to use their illustrations in the volume. I am grateful to Edward Malin for permission to use his drawings of totem pole carvings, and to Karin Clark of Raven Publishing Inc., who graciously allowed us to reproduce line drawings by the late Jim Gilbert. I feel especially honored to include two paintings by the remarkable Tlingit artist Celeste Worl.

The support and enthusiasm of all these people touched me deeply. In addition, I offer special thanks to three people: my friend Kay Smith, of Juneau; Joan K. O'Donnell, my editor, for her sound advice and great patience; and my husband, John, for supporting me through this long process in so many ways.

This book is dedicated to John Howe.

Feeding the Ancestors

Raven guests at a potlatch given by the Kaagwaantaan 32 clan at Sitka, Alaska, in December of 1904. Courtesy American Museum of Natural History, photo 32-8740. E. W. Merrill, photographer.

Tlingit Carved Horn Spoons

Nearly two thousand ethnographic objects—diverse, beautiful, and of great cultural value—make up the Northwest Coast collections at the Peabody Museum of Archaeology and Ethnology. They were fashioned by members of many different tribes living between northern California and southeastern Alaska during the nineteenth century. Acquired by maritime explorers, fur traders, naval officers, Russian colonists, or collectors, they eventually were given to or purchased by the museum.

As has been true for most other Northwest Coast collections, the Peabody's most obviously ceremonial objects—masks, totem poles, rattles, and regalia—have drawn the greatest interest from scholars and art historians.[1] The spoons have attracted little attention, at least partly because they have been categorized as utilitarian, not ceremonial, objects.

Indeed, thirty-five of the 124 spoons in the Peabody's collections are plain, utilitarian wooden spoons and serving ladles. Made of red cedar, red alder, or hemlock, they come in many sizes. The large wooden spoons that I term *ladles* are called *shéen* in the language of the Tlingit people, who made nearly all the spoons now at the

Tlingit utilitarian spoons carved from mountain goat horn, ca. 1840–1865. Collected by Edward Fast, 1867–1868. Top, PM 69-30-10/1753 (L 17 x W 15.1 x D 5.5 cm); bottom, PM 69-30-10/1754 (16.3 x 5 x 4.1 cm). T5042.2. Hillel S. Burger, photographer.

Peabody. (The general term for a spoon in Tlingit is *shál*.)[2] The Tlingits and their neighbors, including the Haidas, used ladles to transfer food from huge serving bowls to smaller, individual bowls, from which a single person ate using a spoon. On the majority of the wooden ladles and spoons, decorative carving is either absent or relatively simple.

Seventy-one Northwest Coast spoons at the Peabody were made from the horns of mountain goats (*Oreamnos americanus*) and Dall sheep (*Ovis dalli*); one spoon is made of antler. The handles of forty-four of the horn spoons are elaborately carved with human and animal figures. The carved spoons, made between about 1840 and 1900, were far more than utilitarian objects. They played vital roles in ceremonies and social functions and served as elaborate records of important events. On their handles artists rendered figures from oral histories and legends as meticulously as they did on the monumental totem poles that scholars have studied so thoroughly. David Katzeek, a Tlingit clan leader and scholar, told me in December 2003: "Our families' histories are carved on these spoons. They show how important it is for Tlingit people to know who they are and how intricately woven the culture of the Tlingit people is."[3]

The ceremonial use of these spoons, their profound association with the ancestors of the Northwest Coast people, and the artistry of their carving make them eminently worthy of closer attention. According to master carver and scholar Bill Holm, these sophisticated objects might be described as the "family silver of Northwest Coast nobility."[4] Although a few of them probably belonged to shamans, most of them must have been made for nobles—people at the top of an extremely hierarchical society that also included commoners and slaves, who had been captured in war from rival groups. Noble families had, through war, marriage, and trade, accumulated great wealth in goods, ceremonial regalia, and crests—emblems or designs that identified a clan or lineage and that, according to anthropologist Frederica de Laguna, were its "most treasured possessions."[5] I have chosen to focus on spoons of the type most likely to have been owned or used by nobles or shamans, because of their great beauty and because of what they can teach us about the Native cultures of the Pacific Northwest Coast.

David Katzeek studying photographs of the Peabody Museum's horn spoons, Juneau, Alaska, December 2002. Katzeek was the first chief executive officer and president of the Sealaska Heritage Institute, which is devoted to the preservation of Tlingit culture. Anne-Marie Victor-Howe, photographer.

I was initially drawn to study this group of spoons because I knew how tremendously difficult it had been for people to obtain the raw materials for them and what great skill the artists had needed to carve them. Later, I became interested in the clan crests that decorate many of them and the stories associated with those crests. I was also attracted by their artistic merit—the carving is of high quality. Because such spoons were used in important ceremonies and memorials, working with them allowed me to become more deeply immersed in Northwest Coast culture. I had already been studying the ways in which Tlingit and Haida people treat their traditional food animals and plants as sacred. The same attitude led them to create and use beautiful utensils with which to serve and eat their food.

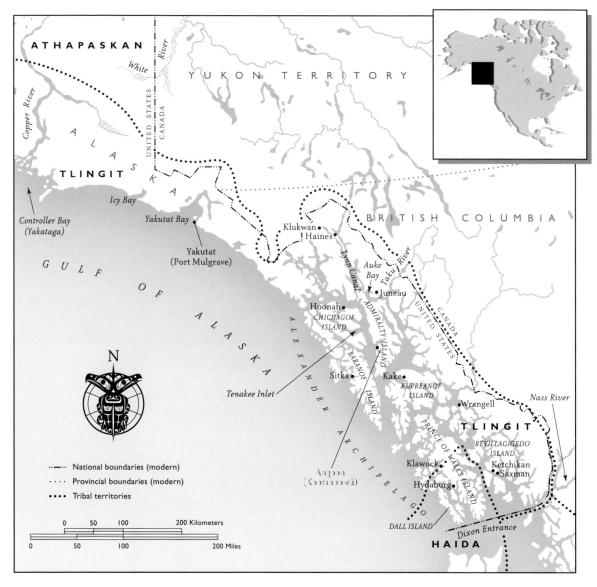

Tlingit and Haida territories in Southeast Alaska. Map by Deborah Reade. Drawing of Eagle/Raven family crest by Jim Gilbert, courtesy Raven Publishing Inc.

From among the carved horn spoons at the Peabody Museum, I selected the twenty-six illustrated in this book, all of which have crests carved on them that represent clans. The spoons are mostly of Tlingit manufacture; only one is almost certainly Haida (pl. 11). They were last used in the mid-nineteenth century by members of tribes in what are today British Columbia and Southeast Alaska, during a time of cultural upheaval when missionaries and American colonists severely restricted the Native ceremonies in which the spoons had been used.

My treatment of these spoons is not art historical. Other writers have already dealt thoroughly with the artistic aspects of Northwest Coast spoons, bowls, and other carved objects.[6] Instead, I am interested in indigenous understandings of the spoons and their meanings—in the power that is inherent in these objects and what they mean from the native perspective. The carvings are deeply related to Tlingit cultural values concerning nature and people's close observation of the animals of land, sea, and sky.

The smaller horn spoons in the collection were each made from a single horn, usually that of a mountain goat but sometimes that of a Dall sheep. A spoon made from mountain goat horn is called *yéts' shál* in Tlingit, and one made from sheep horn is *leineit shál*. Artists inlaid some spoons with abalone shell (*Haliotis kamtschatkana*) for decoration (pls. 9, 12, 18). Larger spoons, made in two pieces, often had bowls fashioned from the translucent amber horns of Dall sheep and handles of mountain goat

Mountain goat (top) and Dall sheep (bottom). Tlingits and Haidas used the horns of the hard-to-hunt mountain goat for cups and gunpowder measures as well as for spoons. The horns of Dall sheep were used to make spoon bowls and large one-piece spoons and ladles. Joel Bennett, photographer.

A Tlingit spoon mold from Chilkat, with a spoon made of mountain goat horn. Tlingit and Haida carved horn spoons were shaped in these wooden molds after being softened in hot water and oil. Courtesy of the Division of Anthropology, American Museum of Natural History, photo 19-1132.

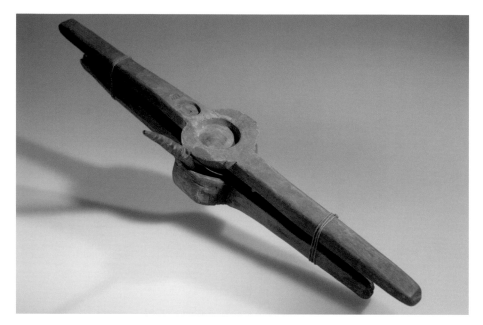

horn (pl. 2), although some were made entirely of goat horn (pl. 5). Before contact with Europeans, the two pieces of these large spoons were fastened together with rivets of mountain goat horn or of copper procured from Athapaskan people (Ahtna and Southern Tutchone) who lived along the Copper and White Rivers. By 1900, people commonly used metal rivets as fasteners (pl. 6). After the Russians introduced cattle to the Northwest Coast in the late 1700s, Tlingit carvers sometimes used cow horn instead of Dall sheep horn to manufacture the largest spoons, and they were making many cow horn spoons for the market by the turn of the twentieth century.[7]

The bowl of a spoon was made by first softening a horn in boiling water, then splitting its broad, hollow base lengthwise and splaying it out. While still warm, the split base was further softened in oil before being lashed into a wooden mold that shaped the bowl. Once dry, it was released from the mold and cut and rounded to form the final bowl shape.

Usually, the narrower top of the horn curved away from the bowl enough to form a handle. If it did not, it was again softened and bent to the desired shape in a mold.

Spoon in a handle-forming jig. Made from a Dall sheep horn, the spoon is carved with an owl and two eagles. It was collected at Klukwan, Alaska, by George T. Emmons. The wooden mold was collected by Emmons at Wrangell, Alaska. Courtesy of the Division of Anthropology, American Museum of Natural History, photo E-311.

Sometimes the same mold was used to shape both bowl and handle. The handle was carved only after the horn had again been softened in warm water. The rough skin of a dogfish (a small shark) was used to polish the final carving. If a spoon with a horn bowl was left in hot liquid, it had to be remolded, so horn spoons were used mostly to eat cool or lukewarm liquids and food. One late-eighteenth-century collector observed that Tlingits usually ate from the side of the spoon, "sucking the more liquid food, and picking out the solid particles with the thumb and forefinger of the other hand."[8]

Generally, the artisans who carved spoons among the Northwest Coast peoples were the same ones who carved similar small objects in argillite, ivory, and bone. The carving is exactly like that on totem poles, but in miniature, and it required the same skill that was demanded of the pole carver. The figure at the top of each spoon handle, like that at the top of a totem pole, was powerfully symbolic. Spoons, however, were especially intimate. Unlike ladles, which merely transferred food from bowl to bowl, spoons made contact with the mouth and—particularly important in Tlingit culture—

the tongue, which was associated with feeding, nurturing, and engendering growth. All the ancestral figures carved on a spoon handle face downward, toward the bowl, so that they are fed when the spoon is filled and a person sips from it. This intimacy between the spoon and the tongue is part of what makes carved spoons such powerful objects in Northwest Coast cultures and different from any other form of carving.

The Tlingits are now the most northerly of the Northwest Coast culture groups, although they once ranged the length of the coast and the islands of the Alexander Archipelago, from Dixon Entrance north to Controller Bay. They lost some of their southernmost land about three hundred years ago when small groups of Haidas from the Queen Charlotte Islands migrated across Dixon Entrance and pushed northward into Tongass Tlingit territory and the southern parts of Prince of Wales Island and Dall Island. In the late eighteenth and early nineteenth centuries the Tlingits themselves expanded north across the Gulf of Alaska to Icy Bay and Controller Bay, taking land from the Athapaskan and Eyak tribes in what is now south-central Alaska. Sometime before the Canada–United States border was formalized in 1906, a group of inland Tlingits who lived along the upper Taku River and elsewhere in southeastern Alaska crossed into Canada and settled in Yukon Territory. The Tlingit language, related to Athapaskan and Eyak, is divided into four areas of differentiated speech: Gulf Coast, Inland, Northern, and Southern.[9]

The Tlingits' neighbors the Haidas, who made one or two of the horn spoons in the Peabody's collection, now live in the Queen Charlotte Islands (Haida Gwaii) off the coast of British Columbia and in the southern portion of the Alexander Archipelago in southeastern Alaska. When the first Europeans arrived in the late eighteenth century, the Haidas occupied settlements on the mainland and near-shore islands of what is today British Columbia and Southeast Alaska. Like Tlingit settlements, each was composed of the houses of one or more matrilineages—descent groups based on the mother's line. The Haida language, with its northern and southern dialects, has no demonstrable relationship to Tlingit and Athapaskan.

Despite their different backgrounds and historical movements, the Tlingits and Haidas share a coastline veined with countless fjords, bays, and rivers and dominated by the cool, wet climate typical of the Pacific Northwest—kept relatively mild by the warming effects of the Japan Current. The mainland shore along this coast is shielded from the ocean by myriad islands and islets. On both mainland and islands, mountains descend steeply to the water's edge. A combination of heavy annual precipitation and acidic soils produces rich, thick vegetation dominated by dense stands of conifers—spruce, hemlock, and cedar. In old-growth forest, the forest floor is carpeted with moss and an understory of shrubs and ferns broken here and there by muskegs, or sphagnum bogs.

In the late 1800s, when most of the spoons pictured in this catalogue were collected, both tribes subsisted primarily on fishing, hunting, and gathering. Following the seasonal cycle from March to November, people fished for salmon and other saltwater and freshwater fish and hunted marine mammals, deer, mountain goats, Dall sheep, seabirds, and migratory waterfowl. They picked berries and wild vegetables, gathered roots, bark, seeds, and other plant foods, and collected birds' eggs and great quantities of shellfish. Ceremonies, with their attendant use of carved horn spoons, took place in the fall and winter.

Among hunters' prized game animals, mountain goats and Dall sheep gave the Tlingits much more than horns from which to craft spoons. According to Joe Hotch, a knowledgeable Tlingit leader of the Kaagwaantaan clan from Klukwan, his ancestors used almost every part of these animals. They ate the meat and fat, forming the fat into cakes, a favorite food that also had value as a trade item among Native people. The tallow, or the fat around the kidneys and in the stomach, served as a medicine for sores, as a

Old-growth Pacific Northwest rainforest on the coast of Southeast Alaska. Western hemlock and Sitka spruce in the Alexander Archipelago can grow to over 150 feet tall and more than three feet in diameter. John Hyde, photographer.

Nathan Jackson and the author in Ketchikan, Alaska, July 2000. Jackson is a widely admired Tlingit carver of monumental poles and other traditional Tlingit wooden objects. He also mentors young carvers and has restored many old poles in southeastern Alaska. John R. Howe, photographer.

hair ointment, and, mixed with melted pitch and charcoal, as a sunscreen for women's faces. The goats' stomachs became buckets in which to carry water while traveling; goat sinew made strong thread; and goatskins served as outer coverings for canoes. From the wool of mountain goats the Tlingits wove *naaxein,* commonly known as Chilkat robes—the five-sided dancing blankets renowned as the "royal robes" of the northern Northwest Coast.[10] They valued the horns for making spoons, gunpowder containers, personal ornaments, charms, and the crowns and headdresses worn by shamans.

Dall sheep were utilized equally thoroughly for their meat, wool, hides, and horns. The largest males weigh up to two hundred pounds and have massive, curled horns, typically some thirty-five inches long, which served well for fashioning the bowls of two-piece spoons and the larger one-piece spoons. The ewes' spike horns are much smaller, less than fifteen inches long.

Raw and processed products from both species made valuable trade items because of the difficulty of obtaining them. Dall sheep and mountain goats live in steep, rocky, mountainous terrain in Alaska and northwestern Canada, where hunting is arduous and risky. They descend to lower elevations only after very heavy snowfalls. The Tlingits hunted them in the fall or early winter when the animals had the most fat and the thickest coats. Before Europeans introduced guns around 1790, Tlingit hunters had only bows and arrows with which to hunt these sure-footed mammals.[11]

The hunters' success is affirmed by the ceremonial horn spoons—among many other objects—in the Peabody Museum's collections. Each spoon hints at who might have used it, how it was used, and which clan owned it. Although long ago people must have been able to "read" the carvings on the spoons and understand their meanings, today much of this knowledge has been lost. Because the collectors of the spoons did not document their origins and meanings, I offer interpretations of them that I obtained through extensive consultation and research with Tlingit and Haida elders, scholars, and carvers. As present-day interpretations, these remarks about crests, stories, and clan ownership are not meant to be definitive. Only those who carved and used the spoons in their own time can be considered true authorities on their meanings and usage.

The entrance to Sitka harbor, 1868, from a contemporary print. Courtesy Argosy Book Store NYC.

THE COLLECTORS

Of the twenty-six spoons illustrated in this book, eighteen were collected by
Edward Fast, a lieutenant in the U.S. Army who was stationed in Sitka, Alaska, from
October 1867 to July 1868. George Thornton Emmons, a navy lieutenant who also
worked out of Sitka, acquired four others. Three known individual collectors and
an unknown one account for the remaining four examples. American mariners such
as Captain Robert Gray and Captain James Magee, who sailed to the Northwest
Coast in the late 1700s, are also known to have collected carved spoons and other
Native artifacts.

One of the most famous Northwest Coast collections at the Peabody Museum was
gathered by Meriwether Lewis and William Clark during their 1804–1806 expedition
to the Pacific Coast and back. Still other collections from the Northwest were donated
by Alice C. Fletcher, F. W. Rindge, and Lewis H. Farlow. Far larger, however, is the
collection of Edward Fast, which the Peabody acquired in 1869.

Emil Teichmann, 1867. Courtesy Argosy Book Store NYC.

EDWARD G. FAST

German by birth, Edward G. Fast was in his early forties when he lived in Sitka. He was known as a quiet man, trained in science, who "kept aloof from the noisy and often rough company of his American colleagues, and consequently had to put up with many jesting or offensive remarks from them, which made his life in the little settlement far from pleasant."[12] Apparently his duties as a lieutenant were limited and left him plenty of free time to get on good terms with some Tlingits and to acquire, with "the assistance of several intelligent and courageous natives," a large collection of what he called "relics."

We would know little about Edward Fast and the methods he used to build his collection of Tlingit artifacts were it not for Emil Teichmann, who, soon after his arrival in Sitka in May 1868, befriended Fast. Teichmann kept a diary of his sojourn in Alaska, which was later published. Then in his twenties, Teichmann worked for the New York branch of J. M. Oppenheim and Company, a leading vendor of furs, based in London. For many years the English firm had maintained a contract with the Russian-American Company for the purchase of Alaska fur seal skins, which were harvested every year in the Aleutian Islands and shipped from Sitka to England. Relations between the two companies began to deteriorate in 1867, after the United States purchased Alaska from Russia. J. M. Oppenheim sent Teichmann to Sitka to check on its business affairs there, notably a missing shipment of furs.

Governor's house, Sitka, 1868.
Drawing by Emil Teichmann.
Courtesy Argosy Book Store NYC.

According to Teichmann, 800 people lived in Sitka in 1867, "of whom 250 were American soldiers and 50 American settlers, whilst the remainder was made up of Russians, Creoles and half-breeds." Sitka's social hierarchy ensured that Fast and Teichmann would move in the same upper-class circles and thus would soon meet. Teichmann recorded in his diary that "the American civil population fell into three classes, which had little to do with each other." The upper class was composed of "the officials of the Quarter-master's Department and of the Customs, the small numbers of municipal authorities, a military chaplain, and finally the Agent of the American Company which, as successor to the Russian Company, was represented in Sitka. . . . The second class, of much lower standing, comprised the traders, keepers of billiard saloons and dealers in spirits." Last, "the population of Sitka was formed by a number of those adventurers who were to be found in all new settlements." Teichmann described these adventurers as "so-called 'Rowdies', professional loafers."[13]

Life in town for the upper class consisted of attending church services, holding tea and whisky parties or "small dances when the weather was bad," and making "small expeditions by sea or land when it is fine." In contrast to this *dolce far niente* lifestyle, the rest of the residents, according to Teichmann, lived in barracks-style structures and spent much of their time in debauchery, drinking, gambling, and prostitution. Neither Fast nor Teichmann had any interest in small dances or tea parties, and even less in drinking and gambling, so perhaps it was inevitable that the two men would spend considerable time together.

Teichmann often visited Fast at his living quarters in the "Castle," the largest and most elegant secular building in town. Formerly the residence of Alexander Baranof, chief manager of the Russian-American Company, it was owned by the United States during Fast's time in Sitka and used as the American officer's club. What immediately struck Teichmann when he called on Fast there was the number of curiosities Fast had accumulated in such a short time. Wall after wall was covered with weapons, swords, masks, headdresses, leather costumes, cuirasses, helmets, and headgear "in the shape of complete animal heads, generally of bears or wolves, though eagles' heads were not uncommon." Many other objects were stacked in Fast's chests and boxes.

Several researchers, including Steve Henrikson, curator of the Alaska State Museum, have questioned the methods Fast used to assemble this ample collection. "Fast's brief tour with the Army, less than one year, would hardly have allowed him to amass such a sizable, diverse, and early collection. While Fast implied that he personally collected all the objects, perhaps his collection consisted partly or wholly of contents of the Russian Museum."[14] This so-called museum comprised the ethnographic and other objects collected by the Russians and left behind when they abandoned their holdings.

Fast used three methods to secure the objects.[15] The first, and by far the most regular and rewarding, was to buy artifacts from local Native intermediaries who brought him items. Teichmann's diary mentions that perhaps the lieutenant's most important source was an old shaman from Sitka who served as his local guide and interpreter.

This man apparently had "considerable influence amongst his fellow tribesmen." Teichmann emphasized that the captain obtained "most of the items in his collection" through this man.

Several times Fast invited Teichmann to his quarters to watch his transactions with the old shaman. "Every morning," Teichmann wrote, "at a fix[ed] time there was a knock at the collector's door and in response to his loud '*chredachschantan*' (come in) [*x'eidei shunatán*, 'open it'] there appeared the tall thin figure of the old scoundrel, wrapped in the usual blanket. With cat-like steps he glided along the wall to the captain's table, blinking at him dubiously, and only after the captain had offered him his hand in greeting and said, '*Yake touthaht, ganu, anchao*' (Good morning, sit down chief) [*Yak'éi ts'ootaat, ganú, aankáau*] did the Indian become reassured and sit down respectfully, drawing his blanket round him in picturesque folds." The old man then asked for a drink. "This was the signal for the collector to produce the usual glass of whisky." After that the captain asked what the old man wanted, and the reply was always the same: "*Chlechlatoa* (I don't want anything) [*Tlél ax tuwáa*]."

When his glass was empty the shaman asked for tobacco and started to smoke. After a long pause, "the crafty old man at last produced, as if by accident, an old piece of carving or some trifle of that kind." But invariably the object produced was not well carved or was of poor quality, and Fast rejected it. Then followed a long silence broken only when the old man at last pulled another object from under his blanket. On one such occasion it was a braid of Indian hair. Most certainly the braid had belonged to a shaman, for they wore their hair long and braided. Fast immediately recognized "what a treasure had been put before him, but he took good care to conceal his pleasure from the native who watched him closely and was quite ready to put up his price in proportion to the captain's eagerness. . . . then ensued a long haggling. . . . Several times the old man picked up the plait and threatened to go away." In the end the captain got the piece he wanted for twenty-five cents. "This transaction was repeated every day."

A second, somewhat less important collecting method employed by Fast was to visit the Indian village on the outskirts of town and purchase objects directly from families.

"They [the Natives] were separated from the town itself by a wooden 18 feet high palisade," Teichmann noted. "About eighty to [one] hundred houses stood there for about a mile and behind the houses on the slope of the hill was one of the burial places." Although American soldiers normally found themselves unwanted in the Tlingit village, Fast managed to gain acceptance. His main duty as an army lieutenant was to produce a topographic map of the area, and the village inhabitants, thinking his survey of their settlement was intended to expand its boundaries, welcomed him. In the end, they won no benefit from the survey.

On several occasions Teichmann joined the lieutenant on his visits to Tlingit households, and he described one such meeting in his diary. The two men were received "with great respect" and were invited to join the Tlingit family around the fire. As usual the captain offered the head of the household a gift of tobacco. Then began a ritual of bargaining similar to that in which Fast and the old shaman regularly faced off. At first the chief brought out for appraisal objects of little value. Fast invariably dismissed them. Eventually the chief got up to fetch the most desirable objects, and the real bargaining began.

The last method Fast used was to raid graveyards, although he acquired none of the spoons illustrated in this book that way. Teichmann recounted one such raid on a small island near Sitka that he said was used only as a burial ground. As Fast and his Tlingit guide silently approached it through the mist, they began to discern several of the deceased's canoes in the trees. It was the Tlingits' custom to leave some of the deceased's belongings, such as canoes and hunting implements for men and cooking pots for women, at the gravesite. Fast and the guide had collected a large quantity of "spoils" from the grave when suddenly the Tlingit threw Fast violently to the ground. He was startled, but after a few seconds his guide silently pointed to a canoe passing by with several Tlingits on board. "Had these Indians seen the desecration of the graves it would have gone very badly with the captain and his guide," Teichmann later wrote. Apparently, after this incident Fast renounced raiding graveyards.

Edward G. Fast acquired cultural objects not because he was interested in Native culture or appreciated Native art but for purely speculative, financial reasons. His collection of some 650 objects would later be exhibited twice commercially, first in San Francisco and then in New York. It would then be placed on sale for $10,000 and finally sold in 1869 for $2,500 to the Peabody Museum.

GEORGE THORNTON EMMONS

The spoons shown in plates 6, 7, 15, and 16 were collected by Lieutenant George Thornton Emmons, a very different man from Edward Fast, with a different attitude toward Tlingit culture. Though an equally zealous collector, Emmons was keenly interested in every aspect of Native culture, despite his lack of

George Thornton Emmons, 1904. As a Navy lieutenant stationed in Alaska in the 1880s and 1890s, Emmons collected thousands of artifacts and much valuable information about traditional Tlingit culture and history. Courtesy American Museum of Natural History, photo 32-8741.

training in ethnography. Besides assembling a large and varied collection, Emmons wrote prolifically and spent much time recording the customs of the inhabitants of the places he visited.

Emmons was born in Baltimore in 1852, graduated from the U.S. Naval Academy in 1874, and in 1882 received his first assignment to Alaska. He, too, was based in Sitka, but unlike Fast, he traveled widely as commanding officer of a ship. In a 1903 letter to the Alaska Boundary Tribunal, he explained his official duties:

> Prior to the establishment of civil government in Alaska, in 1885, the commanding officer of the naval vessel stationed in those waters represented the law supreme; he touched at the native villages, received the chiefs, listened to the complaints of the people, arbitrated and judged the cases, and punished the guilty. Under the orders of the commander, the medical officer of the man-of-war inspected the natives, prescribed for them, and dispensed Government medical stores free. When necessity required, armed detachments were landed from the vessel to preserve order or make arrests. After the establishment of civil law in the Territory the naval commander cooperated with the Government officers to enforce the law and to police the country.[16]

To accomplish his mission, Emmons had to be a skilled diplomat. He ably demonstrated that quality during his first tour of duty in Alaska. Apparently a dispute erupted among the Natives of Áak'w (Auke) village, near present-day Juneau, that resulted in at least one casualty. Arriving on the scene, Emmons, as his first act to restore order, enlisted the services of the "chief," Kaa.wa.ee, who readily cooperated. In a letter Emmons later wrote to *Alaska Magazine*, he said that this action "was the beginning of friendly relations with 'Kowie,'"[17] who would significantly influence Emmons's subsequent investigations into Tlingit culture.

In 1884 Emmons arrived at Sitka aboard the USS *Pinta*, a small gunboat. The *Pinta* was to patrol the waters of southeastern Alaska in order to contain the turmoil resulting from what Emmons described as "the transfer from one governing power to another."[18] Previously the territory had been administered by the U.S. military, but in that year Alaska was transferred to civilian control under an American governor, John Kinkead.

Herring drying on racks in Sitka, 1889. The USS *Pinta*, a gunboat commanded by George T. Emmons, is visible in the background. George T. Emmons, photographer. Courtesy of the Division of Anthropology, American Museum of Natural History.

While commanding the *Pinta*, Emmons also acted as a land surveyor and so was able to collect Native objects from all over southeastern Alaska. In 1886 his duties took him to Port Mulgrave (now Yakutat), where he engaged Native guides to help him gather artifacts. According to Steve Henrikson, he purchased most of these from Tlingit middlemen. From an analysis of Emmons's catalogues and accession notes at the

Peabody Museum and the American Museum of Natural History, Frederica de Laguna, who edited and annotated Emmons's book *The Tlingit Indians*, concluded that "many of the artifacts" Emmons collected "were taken from shaman's graves." None of the spoons illustrated in this book were taken from graveyards, but we do know that one broken spoon at the Peabody Museum and perhaps a few other objects came from graves.

De Laguna stressed in her introduction to Emmons's book that "during the period when Emmons was collecting Tlingit artifacts, the Navy and the missionaries were making their strongest efforts to eradicate the belief in and practice of shamanism."[19] In taking artifacts from shamans' graves, Emmons was conforming to behavioral and ethical norms already well established by many people, mostly Euro-Americans and other foreigners, though prompted by different motivations. Besides missionaries intent on expunging Native religions, there were people like Fast who were engaged in financial speculation. Other collectors valued Native culture and wanted to own objects representative of it; still others merely wanted souvenirs of their excursions to Alaska. The actions of all these people ultimately had the same effect, which was to "divest" the objects of their functions in Tlingit society.[20]

Nevertheless, Emmons was, according to his biographer, Jean Low, "outspoken in defense of the natives" and demonstrated a profound interest in their traditional customs.[21] He befriended many of the Natives he met, and the local people apparently welcomed him warmly. Like other collectors of the time, Emmons may have considered grave robbing a "necessary evil," required to preserve relics of disappearing cultures. Today we view such activities very differently.

By August 1887 Emmons had accumulated as much as three tons of artifacts, ready to be sent to the American Museum of Natural History (AMNH) in New York City, which had encouraged his collecting activities and purchased much of his collection. Ultimately it was an excellent deal for the East Coast museum. Some of the craftsmanship was superb, and some of the items came with good documentation, including their provenance, the name of the previous owner, and a description of the way the object had been used.

In 1887 Emmons obtained a leave of absence from the navy that was subsequently extended to 1891. Freed from his military duties, he had plenty of time to travel around southeastern Alaska, meeting Native people, collecting objects, and recording information. In 1893 the AMNH acquired from Emmons another 2,900 objects "of exceptional value," all of them from Alaska. George Heye, founder of the Museum of the American Indian–Heye Foundation, was another buyer. In 1905 he began dealing extensively with Emmons, acquiring a total of 1,650 objects from him. After that, competition for Emmons's materials among the largest natural history museums—the AMNH, the Field Museum in Chicago, and the Smithsonian Institution's National Museum of Natural History—grew stiff.

From 1891 to 1896, back on duty in the navy, Emmons pursued his collecting and study until he was assigned to duty at the American Museum of Natural History, where he worked on a manuscript about his research in Alaska. Emmons had never enjoyed robust health, and in 1899 his condition worsened to the point that he had to retire from the navy. Nevertheless, he was able to travel frequently to British Columbia and Alaska in the following years, continuing to collect artifacts and document them. By then he was sending collections to institutions other than the AMNH, including the National Museum of Natural History and the Field Museum, which in 1902 purchased 1,400 mostly Tlingit objects. The four feasting spoons illustrated in this book were among 101 objects Emmons sold to the Peabody Museum in 1914. Over the years he sold a total of 334 objects to the Peabody.

In his later years, Emmons, unlike Fast, continued to collect and sell objects even as his sources of supply became fewer and more scattered. According to Jean Low, "he made his last field trip to British Columbia in 1925, but long before that time he would buy large or small lots from a variety of sources, including Victoria and Alaska curio dealers, Miss Sally Ball (former postmistress of Sitka), and L. L. Bales, a prospector who was responsible for most of his Arctic pieces."

In 1932, when he was in his eighties, Emmons moved to Victoria, British Columbia. Despite his declining health, he managed to continue dealing in artifacts for many more years. He died in Victoria of pneumonia on June 11, 1945, at the age of ninety-three.

Interior of Whale House in Klukwan, Alaska, with Tlingit regalia on display, 1895. Also visible is an unusually large carving of a woodworm with a woman's face, probably used as a feast dish. Courtesy Alaska State Library, Winter and Pond, photographers, photo 87-013.

Spoons in Tlingit Culture

The Tlingit people organize themselves into two main groups, which anthropologists call "moieties." Known as the Raven and Eagle sides, they are based on descent in the mother's line (matrilineal kinship). If a woman is born into the Raven moiety, for example, then all her children will be Ravens, too. The moieties structure almost everything in Tlingit social and ceremonial life, which is based on a balance between pairs of counterparts. Members of one moiety call members of the other their "opposites," and marriage to someone of the same moiety traditionally was prohibited. All reciprocal ritual relations, of which the Tlingits have many, are carried out between members of opposite moieties.

Each moiety in turn encompasses twenty to twenty-five clans, although not every clan is represented in every community. Historically, clan members shared rights to fishing, hunting, and gathering places. They also owned village sites and symbolic properties such as names, songs and dances, certain ceremonial privileges, stories and

The Gaanax̱.ádi Raven Pole, Sitka National Historical Park, Sitka, Alaska, 2002. This figure, which appears at the bottom of the pole, is a yellow hawk, *gijook*, also called "Golden Eagle," a crest owned by the Gaanax̱.ádi and several other Tlingit clans. Anne-Marie Victor-Howe, photographer.

legends that explained the clan's origins, and crests. Crest ownership, however, was not exclusive; more than one clan could "own" rights to the same crest symbol. Within a village, each clan had one main house, which was the house of the clan leader—the wealthiest or most powerful member of the clan in that community. Nobles, commoners, and shamans all belonged to clans, although shamans were outsiders in a sense, generally living in the forest outside the villages. Every big clan had at least one shaman, who was paid for his or her work.

Tlingit clans are further subdivided into descent groups that anthropologists call "matrilineages." Tlingits know them as "house groups," because traditionally their members lived together in one large, communal house. Even today, when lineage members may live in dispersed residences, each house group has a leader and a name, such as Bear House, Frog House, or Wolf House. Some of the names, though not all, are the names of crest animals that belong to the matrilineage.

Both the tangible and the intangible property owned by a clan is termed *at.óow*, meaning, literally, "an owned or purchased thing or object." According to Nora Marks Dauenhauer and Richard Dauenhauer, widely respected experts on Tlingit culture, "this fundamental concept [*at.óow*] underlies all dimensions of Tlingit social structure, oral literature, iconography, and ceremonial life."[22] Anthropologist Sergei Kan described *at.óow* as "named entities or objects," usually animals. Only the matrilineal groups that own *at.óow* have the right to represent them symbolically on totem poles, the fronts of houses, certain items of clothing, and other objects such as carved spoons.[23] As Steve Henrikson told me, however, "not everything with a crest image is *at.óow*—only things brought out and named before the opposite side [during ceremonies], with gifts going to the witnesses, and a caretaker appointed to watch over them." The clan crests carved on the Peabody's horn spoons were probably *at.óow*, and the spoons themselves would have been considered *at.óow* when they were used in ceremonial contexts.

At.óow were originally acquired by members of the nobility and shamans as the result of actual historical events, in dreams associated with historical events, or in visions of ancestors who encountered beings in animal form and received supernatural powers from them. According to David Katzeek, *at.óow* demonstrate a Tlingit clan's wealth, both spiritual and material. If someone has the right spirits on his side, material goods come to him easily. Ownership of clan and lineage property was transferred when that property was given to a member of another clan or lineage as a ceremonial or marriage gift, indemnity for an injury or loss of life, collateral on a debt, war booty, or part of a peace settlement.[24]

Traditionally, the owner of an item of symbolic property commissioned someone from the opposite moiety to manufacture or create objects depicting or representing that *at.óow*. Because the Peabody Museum spoons were all carved during the nineteenth century, it is probably safe to assume that, in accordance with this practice, they were made by members of the moiety opposite to the one that owned the spoon and the crest carved on it. More recently, it has become possible for members of a moiety to manufacture their own *at.óow* objects and to commission them from members of the same moiety. Again, the object becomes *at.óow* only after a ceremonial dedication. When someone who serves as a trustee for the *at.óow* dies, the object is still *at.óow* but is now identified as *l s'aatí át,* a "masterless" *at.óow,* until a new steward can be designated.[25]

Because even the most powerful house owned only a certain number of crests, not every spoon or other object could be unique in design—some carved objects had to be duplicated. Several spoons, generally made by the same carver, might look exactly alike. One scholar of Northwest Coast art explained that "spoons were often made in sets which were kept together and used only on special occasions."[26] During a ceremony held in 2004 in Sitka by the Wolf House of the Kaagwaantaan clan to commemorate the hundredth anniversary of the "last potlatch"—held in the same town by three Kaagwaantaan Wolf Houses in 1904—I had the opportunity to see such a set of spoons on display among other regalia belonging to the clan.

Crests are among the most important kinds of *at.óow*, and one cannot understand Tlingit carved spoons without understanding what the crests on them mean. According to Frederica de Laguna, these emblems "represented [a clan or lineage's] totems, that

The G̱aanax̱.ádi Raven Pole, Sitka National Historical Park, Sitka, Alaska, 2002. Carved by Nathan Jackson and Steve Brown, the pole is a reproduction of an older pole collected in the Tlingit village of Tuxekan, on Prince of Wales Island. According to Jackson, the Raven and Whale story depicted on the pole is also represented on the spoon in plate 18. Anne-Marie Victor-Howe, photographer.

is, certain animals, birds, fish, and invertebrates, heavenly bodies, prominent land-marks, and even ancestral heroes and certain supernatural beings associated with them."[27] Contemporary Tlingit political leader and scholar Rosita Worl summarized the social and spiritual purposes of these complex visual symbols:

> They identify a clan and its membership. They distinguish its clan members apart from others and define relationships to other Tlingit. Crests chronicle the origin or other supernatural and significant events in the history of a clan. They serve a legal function in recording a clan's title to the object on which the crest is placed and the site and geographic region where the event occurred. . . . crests symbolize the special relationship between a clan and the animal depicted on the crest. Crests, the associated oral tradition, songs, and names represent real and intellectual property that is owned by clans. They are also property which clans protected most vigorously.[28]

Thus the property dimensions of objects that feature crests include outright clan ownership of the objects; the rights of clan members to handle the objects; ownership of the crests depicted on the objects and the right to reproduce them; and a propri-etary relationship with the spirits depicted and embodied in the crests.

Many different figures enliven the handles of the spoons at the Peabody Museum, including human beings, humanlike figures, the spirits of animate and inanimate objects, and representations of natural phenomena such as the moon, the sun, clouds, thunder (pl. 4), mountains, rocks, and islands. Because most Tlingit and Haida crests are figures of animals, most of the crests carved on the spoons portray animals (pls. 8, 10). Both Tlingits and Haidas see all animals, and especially those represented in crests, as similar to humans in many ways. They believe animals live in villages similar to human settlements, have souls, can talk among themselves and understand human speech, and can easily change back and forth between human and animal form. These beliefs are manifested in the countless stories and legends people tell about animals.

Each crest animal maintains its physical and behavioral characteristics in the supernatural world, and the humans who own the crest are believed to share those

Guests at a commemoration ceremony in Sitka, Alaska, 2004, display their Raven regalia and *at.óow*. Visible are drums, wooden hats, and Chilkat robes. A carving of a beaver can be seen in the middle foreground. Photo by James Poulson, *Daily Sitka Sentinel.*

attributes. For example, four of the spoons in the Peabody Museum feature the brown bear (pls. 14, 19, 20, 21), and one depicts a man wearing a headdress with bear ears (pl. 22). This animal is perceived to be very powerful, both physically and intellectually. People who belong to the Teikweidí clan, whose main crest animal is the bear, are believed to have the bear's strength and courage.[29] Because of the bear's

Brown bear (*Ursus arctos midden-dorffi*), Admiralty Island, Southeast Alaska. The Alaska coastal brown bear is a powerful crest animal for the Tlingit, who call it "Chief of the Woods." Anne-Marie Victor-Howe, photographer.

long months of dormancy during hibernatation, it is also thought to possess great knowledge of the non-human spiritual world, and it could be a powerful spirit helper to shamans.

Disappearing into the earth in the autumn and reemerging in the spring, the bear became a powerful symbol of death and rebirth. Its isolation and fasting in a dark, remote den resembled the Tlingits' own practices during initiations, including puberty rites and shamans' initiations.

Bears' physical resemblance to humans is also seen as evidence of their close relationship with humans. Their skinned carcasses resemble human corpses; they stand up on their hind legs like humans; and they use their front paws like hands, with great dexterity. Many Tlingit stories emphasize the importance of respecting bears in order not to offend them and risk losing the power they can transfer to humans. When addressing bears, Tlingits use circumlocutions, metaphoric or kinship terms, and honorific names, referring to them, for example, as "those animals that walked" or "those great inland animals." A woman who encounters a bear in the woods might address it as "my brother" or ask it to "pity me, my big father." Lest a Tlingit hunter offend the bears and drive them away, he never says to another person that he is hunting bears, but only that he is going for a walk in the woods. De Laguna reported that bears were believed to be able to read people's thoughts.[30]

Besides depicting whole animals, the spoons frequently display human and animal faces (pls. 10, 13). This is because, for the Tlingits, the head is the most important part of the body. Humans are born headfirst—face first—and obviously cannot take their first breath without the head. The head is also the highest point of the body, closest to the spirit world. During ceremonies, particularly during the postfuneral ceremony that I discuss later, people "bring out" and witness the dedication of crest objects, including spoons, the designs of which give special representational attention to facial features such as mouths, tongues, teeth, eyes, noses, and ears.

Portrayals of various beings devouring each other are also common on the horn spoons in the Peabody collections, as they are on many other Pacific Northwest Coast objects. The digestive cycle, from eating to excreting and even vomiting, is an important part of the vital force of both humans and animals. It is often depicted on crest objects and emphasized in the stories associated with them. In two versions of the story "The Woman Who Married the Bear," recorded by Dauenhauer and Dauenhauer, a woman steps in bear excrement while picking berries.[31] She makes an uncomplimentary remark about bears, and a bear hears her and is offended. He captures her and marries her, although in the end he is killed by her brothers.

Regardless of their crest designs, Tlingit ceremonial spoons were inherently linked to eating and digesting, to the mouth and tongue. Noble families brought them out, displayed their crests, and offered them to their guests for use in feasting during the *ḵoo.éex'*, the ceremony commonly known as the potlatch. A closer look at the *ḵoo.éex'* yields a clearer picture of the role spoons once played in Tlingit social life.

Graveyard at Howkan, Alaska, 1897. Shown (left to right) are traditional carvings of a killer whale, an eagle, and a bear. A more recent grave house made from commercially manufactured wood is visible in the background. Courtesy Alaska State Library, Winter and Pond, photographers, photo 87-058.

Spoons in Ceremonial Use

The *koo.éex'* is the most important and elaborate of Tlingit ceremonies. Its name derives from the Tlingit verb stem for "to call" or "to invite"—that is, to invite participation in a ceremony.[32] Its common name, "potlatch," derives from Chinook jargon, a language of trade that developed from a Nun-chah-nulth (Nootka) source. Hosted by wealthy, high-status families, potlatches were "elaborate ceremonies and feasts at which a wide variety of announcements, proclamations and initiation rites were performed and communicated."[33] The occasions that called for potlatches included new house dedications, totem pole raisings, and postfuneral memorials. Carved horn spoons were among the clan-owned goods, or *at.óow*, that were used ceremonially during potlatches.

Tlingit people still hold *koo.éex'* frequently. Although the ceremony has evolved somewhat over the years, it remains one of the most significant means by which they express important features of their traditional culture. For historical accuracy, however, and to show how the ceremonial spoons illustrated in this book might have been used, I look exclusively at the *koo.éex'* as they were performed before the mid-nineteenth century.

Tlingit guests landing canoes along the Chilkat River in southeastern Alaska, 1895. The guests are about to attend a ceremony, probably a *koo.éex'*, and likely are singing as the hosts, wearing regalia, welcome them. Courtesy Alaska State Library, Winter and Pond, photographers, photo 87-043.

Specifically, I look at the most important of them, the postfuneral ceremony and feast held to commemorate the dead.

The largest memorial ceremonies took place one to several years after the death of a high-ranking Tlingit. They were hosted by relatives of the deceased on his or her mother's side. The guests belonged to the moiety opposite that of the deceased. Most *koo.éex'* were performed in the fall or winter, after the summer's work had provided plenty of food.

The ceremony's primary purpose was, and still is, to mourn and honor the deceased and to comfort the deceased's clan. It also served to repay members of the opposite moiety who had performed services associated with the funeral and wake, such as cleaning and dressing the body. During the four-day ceremony, the spirits of the deceased and all the late members of his or her matrilineal kin were believed to be present, feasting and celebrating with the living.[34] At these times the high-caste members of both moieties used the hosts' ceremonial horn spoons both actually, for serving and eating food during feasting, and symbolically, as a way of "feeding the ancestors." When a guest ate from a spoon, the ancestors and crest animals represented on the spoon's handle shared in the nourishment.

Sergei Kan stressed that whereas the funeral itself had been centered on the deceased—that is, on the preparation and cremation of the body—the ḵoo.éex' "was an opportunity for the hosts to memorialize, honor, and please all the departed matrikin." At the same time, the guests "represented and incarnated their own matrilineal ancestors, whose names they carried and whose regalia they wore."[35] Their role as mediators between the living and dead was enhanced by their use of objects that had also been used by the deceased and his or her ancestors. The guests sat on mats that had once belonged to the mothers and maternal uncles of the hosts, and they ate from wooden bowls using horn spoons with which the deceased and his or her maternal kin had once eaten.[36]

Horn spoons were integral features of the second part of the ḵoo.éex'. The first part, the mourning, was always a somber event that included a performance re-creating the funeral. After the hosts made welcoming speeches to the guests, the guests assisted the hosts in dressing in their most sacred lineage- and clan-owned regalia. This was the first time since the funeral that the regalia had been worn by the deceased's living descendants, and the clothing and paraphernalia were believed to retain part of the deceased's social persona and to represent his or her matrilineal ancestors.[37]

Next came grieving songs, or crying songs, gaax̱, for the departed, the most valuable of which referred to the mourners' crests.[38] The songs were accompanied by drumming on drums painted with crests. Dances were performed during this part of the ceremony, too.

When the crying songs for the departed were over, someone from the guest group asked permission to speak. Then, whether the deceased was a man or a woman, the guests conducted the l s'aatí sháa gaax̱í, which can be translated as "widow's cry." It consisted of songs, speeches, and the display of at.óow, including carved spoons, for the removal of grief and sorrow from the hosts, the mourning moiety. As Dauenhauer and Dauenhauer put it: "When [Tlingit] people are in grief, others come to console them by telling them of their own losses. The at.óow displayed by the

These mortuary poles stood in
front of the house of Chief Shakes
VI in Wrangell, Alaska, ca. 1895.
G̲unakadeit, a sea monster, is
carved on the pole to the left. The
pole on the right displays a brown
bear. The ashes of the chief's father
and mother were in the G̲unakadeit
pole, and the bear pole held the
ashes of his brother. Courtesy
Alaska State Library, Winter and
Pond, photographers, photo 87-115.

guests communicate the loss of relatives shared
through the kinship system by hosts and guests. . . .
This is another example of [the] 'balance' or reci-
procity through . . . mutual supporting of each other"
that is basic to Tlingit culture and social structure.[39]

During the display of *at.óow*, the crests on the
objects took on special importance as they brought
back memories of the dead. (A contemporary display
of *at.óow* can be seen in the foreground of the photograph on page 31.) Kan described the crests as "towels
for wiping the mourners' tears, blankets to warm
them, supports to help them stand up, containers for
catching their tears and preventing them from falling
on the floor, and armor to equip them for battle."[40] In
short, the widow's cry served to comfort the mourners,
to reiterate that death was not going to destroy the
harmony and balance of Tlingit society, to facilitate
the interaction of ancestors with their descendants,
and to raise the status of the speakers—the guests—
and their matrilineal group.

The hosts concluded the widow's cry ceremony
with speeches of gratitude to the guests and asked
the *naa káaní*, the brothers-in-law of the deceased, to remove their grief with four
chants. The grieving stage was then over, and the more joyous part of the *k̲oo.éex'*
began. During the remainder of the ceremony, participants were occupied with
distributing gifts, singing happy, light-hearted songs, dancing, joking, flirting, and
much eating. This was where horn spoons came into play.

The food presented during the postfuneral ceremony was always abundant and
varied. It might include the meat of bears, mountain goats, deer, moose, seals, and sea
lions, together with seal fat, herring eggs, salmon, halibut, black cod, and hooligan—
eulachon, or *saak* (*Thaleichthys pacificus*), an anadromous smelt. Invariably the hosts

served a variety of berries and large amounts of seal oil and hooligan oil. The food and oil were brought to the feast in large wooden dishes or sometimes in very large spoons decorated with crests. It was then dished into smaller bowls for each person with decorated ladles or large spoons made of wood or horn. Each implement was used for a certain kind of food or liquid. Bill Holm tells us that "elaborately sculptured spoons and ladles were reserved for formal occasions [such as this] when the display of the family myths and crests on their handles was appropriate."[41]

According to Cecilia Kunz, a knowledgeable Tlingit elder from the L'uknax.ádi clan of the Raven moiety, whom I interviewed in March 2002, a person of high status would have owned several ceremonial bowls and spoons. Together, members of the various local lineage houses belonging to the same clan as the host helped provide all the decorated bowls and spoons to be used in a potlatch. In order to invite many guests, therefore, a house had to be powerful, with an abundance of carved objects to present to the guests for their use.

Cecilia Kunz at a celebration in her honor, Juneau, Alaska, 2003. A L'uknax.ádi from the Raven moiety, Kunz has been influential in reviving the Tlingit language. Anne-Marie Victor-Howe, photographer.

Besides the social feasting, a more serious part of the *koo.éex'* involving food and eating took place during this stage of the ceremony. This was the "feeding of the dead," a ritual in which food and water were offered "to all of the dead members of one's matrilineal group, [who were] believed to be present in the house during the entire ceremony."[42] The food was displayed in what is called the "fire dish," *gankas'ix'i.* One way to symbolically feed the deceased was to place the food in the fire. That way it was "transferred through the fire to a specific individual who had been named in the ceremony."[43] Another way was for the hosts to feed their guests by hand by placing a little food directly into the guest's mouth.[44]

The displayed food was then placed in bowls. Guests ate the solid food using their hands and drank the oil from spoons. By eating food given to them by the hosts and using the hosts' utensils, decorated with the hosts' crests, the guests not only nourished the deceased but also reassured them that they still had standing in society and remained valued members of their clan.

Hooligan oil held special significance for the Tlingits. Martha Betts, who studied the Tlingit hooligan fishery at Klukwan and Haines, Alaska, in 1990 and 1991, reported that hooligan oil was not only a food but also "a medicinal product drunk to cure ailments such as arthritis, tuberculosis and cancer." Tradition maintains that it has value as a barometer, an indicator of both weather changes and social or personal events. Tlingit elders told Betts that "the personality of hooligan," and by extension that of people who owned the hooligan as a crest animal, was "defined by happiness, contentment, and sensitivity to their surroundings." Moreover, according to a story told to Betts by Austin Hammond, a leader of the Lukaax̱.ádi clan in Haines, "daylight, introduced to the world by Raven, [was] the source of the hooligans' spiritual power. . . . hooligan are as essential to survival as is daylight itself."[45]

Thus, when drinking hooligan oil from their hosts' decorated horn spoons, the guests at a ḵoo.éex' not only fed themselves but also nourished the deceased, giving him what he needed for his long, difficult, final journey to his "future life" in the land of the spirits: plenty of nourishment, medicine to cure his ailments, a barometer to show him the weather ahead, light to show the way, spiritual power for survival, and happiness and contentment.

Spoons, then, played an important role in memorial ḵoo.éex' in a very immediate way. When the host gave a spoon filled with oil or other food to the guest, both the guest and the ancestors represented on the spoon received nourishment. All the figures carved on the spoon's handle faced downward, toward the bowl, so that they were fed when the spoon was filled. The story represented by the carvings could actually "eat" the food or oil when the guest ate or sipped it. By eating food—some of it the favorite food of the deceased—with implements displaying the hosts' crests, the guests helped feed the ancestors and comfort them with the spirits depicted on the spoons. When used in memorial potlatches, carved horn spoons served as intimate links between the living and the dead.

Spoons and Shamans

Tlingit shamans, or *íxt'*, may have owned three of the spoons in the Peabody's collections (pls. 11, 24, 25). The handle of one of them (right, and pl. 25) portrays what appears to be a shaman wearing a headdress crowned with mountain goat horns, indicating clearly that the spoon was owned by a shaman. The shaman figure is coupled with images of an otter (*Lutra canadensis*) and an octopus. (Tlingits, when speaking in English, generally use the term *land otter* [*kooshdaa*] rather than *river otter*, to distinguish this animal from the sea otter.) An octopus also appears on the spoon pictured in plate 11, and a land otter, along with a raven, decorates the spoon in plate 24 (see also p. 42). The Tlingits associated all these animals with shamans, though they also served as crest animals for clans.

Some spoons owned by shamans (who could be either male or female) were carved with images of supernatural beings, or *yéik*. Acquired during a shaman's spirit quest, a *yéik* was "a disembodied spirit or supernatural power that reveals itself to a shaman and comes to the shaman as helper."[46] A shaman

Handle of Tlingit shaman spoon
depicting a land otter and a raven.
PM 69-30-10/1745. T5112.1.
Hillel S. Burger, photographer.
See also plate 24.

served as a medium for spirits, and great shamans were said to have had as many as eight spirits that they could call.[47] A spirit did not appear in the natural world of its own volition but was summoned by the shaman, who, during a shamanic ritual, was himself transformed into a spirit. In trance, shamans could travel almost anywhere in both physical and spiritual form, often to remote, inaccessible places—even under-water.

Among the main duties of a Tlingit shaman were to cure patients and to ensure the well-being of his or her clan. Shamans did not administer medicines or treat patients physically but instead, through the power of their spirit helpers, determined the nature of the illness, identified its cause, named those responsible for it, and exor-cised it.[48] They assisted at difficult childbirths and were believed to be able to change the weather. Shamans advised clan leaders, especially when war parties were being mounted, and they performed rituals and ceremonies to bring their people large runs of fish and abundant game. Rosita Worl noted that especially during Tlingit winter ceremonies, the shaman called his spirits "to protect the clan from hostile and dan-gerous spirits."[49] Anatolii Kamenskii, a Russian Orthodox missionary who live in Sitka between 1895 and 1898, wrote that "in the old days of paganism, a shaman would only serve the clan in one tribe. Rarely would neighboring, related, or friendly clans use his services. In the latter case, the shaman had to have power and enormous prestige and to be of noble origin."[50]

The Tlingits whom I consulted for this study were unanimous that shamans did not use decorated spoons like the ones illustrated in this book while curing patients. They may have used them often in their everyday lives, however, because, as de Laguna observed, diet was important for the shaman and his or her spouse. Some food, especially shellfish, was taboo or could be eaten only at certain times of the year. The shaman used only his own dishes, and "all of his personal possessions had a more or less sacrosanct character and were probably never handled by others, except at times by assistants who shared his taboos."[51] Moreover, a shaman's paraphernalia, includ-ing spoons and other implements, helped to connect him with his spirits, who were believed to reside in such shamanic objects. Although shamans did not use spoons during curing rituals, they may have used them ritually when preparing for a battle

or a spirit quest. Oral history and interviews with Tlingit elders and scholars
support the conclusion that these spoons
were used in a ritual manner.

As depicted on the spoon in plate 25
(and see p. 41), Tlingit shamans often
wore headdresses crowned with mountain
goat horns to protect themselves during
their dangerous journeys to distant
realms. Like a shaman on a spirit quest
to faraway lands, mountain goats roam
distant, inaccessible places high in the
mountains. They use their daggerlike horns to protect themselves against predators
and, during the rutting season, to joust with rival males. Aurel Krause, a German
geographer who, with his brother Arthur, spent six months among the Tlingits in the
winter and spring of 1881–1882, noted that a shaman wore such a headdress during
a curing ceremony in 1882 at a camp belonging to a clan in Hoonah, a village on
Chichagof Island, Alaska: "On a mat beside the fire sat the patient, a five-year-old
boy, and at his side was a shaman who looked very old with graying hair that hung in
thick strands to his knees. On his head he wore a crown of wooden sticks, bent to
resemble the horns of the mountain goat, which rattled as they struck each other
through his movements."[52]

Octopi, portrayed on the spoons in plates 11 and 25, similarly have physical and
behavioral qualities that appealed to shamans, especially their ability to transform
themselves. The giant Pacific octopus (*Octopus dofleini*), found in the waters of
southeastern Alaska and called *náakw* in Tlingit, is one of the largest octopods. It can
reach up to 270 kilograms in weight, and its arms can be up to five meters long. When
necessary it can constrict its body to enter extremely narrow crevices in rocks, and it
can quickly change the color and texture of its skin to blend in with its surroundings
and elude predators. When disturbed, it often releases a cloud of blue-black ink as a
decoy that enables it to escape without being followed.[53]

Mountain goat in steep terrain.
Like a shaman on a spirit quest to
faraway lands, the mountain goat
roams distant, inaccessible places
high in the mountains. Joel Bennett,
photographer. Drawing of mountain goat by Jim Gilbert, courtesy
Raven Publishing Inc.

Other octopus behavior, too, suggests shamanic acts and rituals. For example, octopi possess strong weapons for hunting, including venom that they use to anaesthetize their prey. An octopus can grab a crab with one arm and crack the shell with its short, powerful beak or drill a hole in it with the rasped tip of its tongue, in order to suck out the meat. Tlingit shamans used a similar technique when they sucked the disease out of a sick person with a "soul catcher"—a hollow cylinder of finely carved bone, often from a brown bear. At both ends of many Tlingit soul catchers are representations of animals' mouths.

The Haidas, like the Tlingits, strongly associated octopi with shamanism. In a Haida story that takes place on Prince of Wales Island, for example, a woman of the Raven moiety goes by canoe to gather roots and fails to return. Her relatives find only her empty canoe floating on the water. The village shaman then learns that she is living with the Octopus people in their underwater village. People feel reassured, knowing that she is still alive. Later, the shaman has to intervene when the Octopus people attack the Raven people in revenge for some human children's mistreatment of a baby octopus. The octopi are forced to retreat, and the Raven chief gives a big potlatch in honor of the Octopus people, the Raven woman, and the baby octopus. Peace between the Raven people and the Octopus people is once again secured.[54]

Like the mountain goat and the octopus, the land otter—portrayed on the spoons in plates 24 and 25—had special powers that made it dangerous to humans. Only shamans, by using many precautions, could approach and conquer these animals, which were believed to capture people who drowned in the sea or became lost in the forest. Tlingit legends abound with tales of land otters, mostly portraying them as harmful to common people, although occasionally they cast otters as compassionate and grateful to humans who treat them kindly. The caption for plate 25 summarizes two examples.

Land otters can change easily back and forth between human and otter form. The sinuous, supple grace of otters swimming underwater lent them an otherworldly quality in the eyes of Tlingits. To them, Sergei Kan pointed out, any animal that moved like that was suspect, because bones were the essence of the living form, hardening with maturity and lasting even after death and cremation to maintain some essence of the living person. "The notion that the bones constituted the major material component as well as the blueprint of the body is also supported by the frequent use of the skeletal or 'X-ray' image in Tlingit art. . . . The bones underneath the skin are depicted on many representations of crests as well as on shamanic paraphernalia."[55] In the carving of the land otter shown in plate 25, the animal's ribs are clearly articulated.

A story published by ethnographer John R. Swanton in 1909 illustrates the dangerous qualities of the land otter.[56] A long time ago, several men from Sitka went on a canoe trip, and all but one of them drowned. That one was rescued by some land otters, who took him in their canoe to a land otter village a great distance away. There the man found a relative of his who had drowned and now was the wife of two land otters. She told him that her husbands might be able to save him. They brought the man back to Sitka, traveling on a big sea skate, and dropped him off at his village at night. The people there saw that the man was now part human and part land otter, so they captured him with a rope snare and tried to turn him back into the person he had been before the accident. Eventually the man recovered part of his former self, but he was still wild and could consume only raw food. One day he tried to eat a little piece of cooked food and dropped dead immediately.

Octopus. Drawing by Edward Malin from his *Totem Poles of the Pacific Northwest Coast,* fig. 67.

Land Otter was always the first being to appear to a novice shaman. Although dangerous, its magical qualities could assist the shaman on his or her journey. Anthropologist Aldona Jonaitis wrote that "the shaman has two options for handling it: he can try to conquer it, as he does the witch; or he can try to coerce it to work for him, rather than against him."[57] Often he did so by cutting out the otter's tongue, tying it in a bundle made of two pieces of wood, and hiding it away in the woods in a cave or a hollow tree. It was then safe for the shaman to encounter other animals, including the bear. Some particularly powerful Tlingit shamans had as many as eight otter tongues hidden away like this.[58]

Anatolii Kamenskii stressed that the shaman's most difficult task was to obtain a land otter's tongue:

> Prior to the coming of white people to Alaska, when the Tlingit were afraid of committing the sin of killing their fellow man in the guise of a land otter, there were plenty of these animals everywhere, and one could encounter them on any island. Hence a candidate for shamanism could easily meet a land otter, but was not allowed to kill it with any weapon. He could not even use a stone or stick but had to rely on the power of his word. He had to come close to the land otter and kill it by uttering the sound 'o' in various tones. A powerful shaman made the land otter fall flat on its back, with its tongue sticking out, and die after the first utterance. The tongue was what the shaman was after. He cut it out, while uttering various sacred formulae, and had to keep it for the rest of his life, carrying it on his chest.[59]

For the Tlingit people, the tongue was "the container of the life force" for all creatures. Extended tongues that penetrated mouths and orifices transferred powers from one being to another or united them as one being.[60] Because tongues were essential to speech, they symbolized important social functions. Along with the mouth and teeth they were intrinsic to eating and drinking and thus to life itself. Finally, extended tongues symbolized sexual activity.[61]

Another animal depicted on one of the probable shaman spoons in the Peabody collection (pl. 11) is the sculpin, or bullhead (*tlóox*), a fish of the family Cottidae. It, too, belongs to the supernatural domain and was sacred to shamans. This carnivorous bottom fish has a broad, flat head, a large, downturned mouth, and sharp pectoral fins. It lives in deep, cold water and, like the octopus, can change color to blend in with its surroundings. Tlingits and Haidas did not prize sculpins as food, but shamans appreciated them for their supernatural powers. They were said to carry shamans on their strong backs and to help secure bigger fish runs and ensure better weather. Their bodies are partly covered with scales that resemble the armor worn by Tlingit warriors, which no doubt increased the protection they offered for shamans on dangerous journeys to faraway realms.

A final animal that must be mentioned in connection with Tlingit shamanism is the raven, even though it appears on none of the Peabody spoons that may have belonged to shamans. It does appear on several other spoons (pls. 17 and 18). The raven is a crest animal frequently portrayed on the ceremonial regalia of members of the Raven moiety, but it is also associated with shamanism and among the Tlingits was sometimes used by shamans of the Eagle moiety. Raven, or *yéil*, is a supernatural being who created the world as it is now, with its humans and animals, mountains and oceans, moon and sun. When John Swanton recorded the cycle of Raven stories in 1904 at Wrangell, Alaska, the leader of the Kaasx̱'agweidí clan of the Raven moiety told the story of a man without arms who was cured by Raven when the latter transformed himself into a shaman. The story explained "how the Tlingit came to have shamans." On another occasion, Raven entered a house where a man had just died. "So he raised the dead man's blanket with both hands, held it over the body and brought him back to life."[62]

In short, just as Tlingit nobles had their family crests and mythological ancestors carved on the handles of their best spoons, so shamans had carvings of their spirit helpers and other emblems of their calling. Each helper provided different powers, senses, and physical abilities that allowed the shaman to make many arduous journeys to the spirit world and back.

Raven with sun (top) and sculpin. Drawings by Jim Gilbert, courtesy Raven Publishing Inc.

Two Spoons and Their Stories

Although all the spoons in this collection merit attention, two are of particular interest because of the quality of their carving and the fact that the stories and crests associated with them are well known. The first is the spoon illustrated in plate 3, the handle of which depicts the legendary character Dukt'ootl'—Blackskin or Strong Man—who is said once to have torn a sea lion in half (see also pl. 1).

In a version of the Blackskin story recorded by Viola Garfield, a hunter is killed by a sea lion.[63] He is carried home by his hunting partner, who vows that someday the hunter's nephews will kill the sea lion with their bare hands. Everyone trains hard to prepare for the fight. Two young men who are particularly strong plan a contest for the men of the village in which they have to pull a branch off an old, dry tree and pull up a live spruce by its roots. Everybody tries, but no one succeeds.

In the village lives a man whom everyone mocks and accuses of being lazy. He trains secretly in the evening, when it is cold and all the other men have returned to the village, by standing in icy water until he is almost frozen. When he gets home he

Inside the Frog House of the G̲aanax̲teidí clan of Klukwan, ca. 1895. The pole on the left shows Cannibal clutching an emaciated child who is half frog, half human. The house post on the right displays the Frog crest. Courtesy Alaska State Library, Winter and Pond, photographers, photo 87-017.

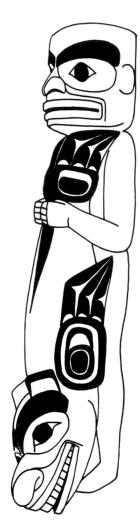

A drawing of Strong Man (Dukt'ootl' or Blackskin) and sea lion, by Edward Malin. The two figures are carved on the spoon in plate 3. Courtesy Edward Malin, from his *Totem Poles of the Pacific Northwest Coast*, fig. 110.

lies down in warm ashes. Because he is so dirty all the time, everyone calls him Blackskin. One night while Blackskin is standing in the water, a small man calls to him and tells him, "I am Strength; I am the Strength of the North Wind. Come and try to throw me." They wrestle on the beach. Soon Strength throws Blackskin to the ground and tells him to continue training.

Many days later Blackskin again wrestles the small man on the beach, and this time he wins. Strength tells him that now he is ready to return to the village and pull the spruce tree up by its roots. Blackskin does as he is told and succeeds. Strength then tells him to go to the other end of the village, where the old tree stands, and pull off a limb. Blackskin succeeds again. He then urinates in the place where the limb had been attached and reattaches it. Strength tells him that now he is even stronger than the north wind and is ready to fight.

The next morning, the two strongest men of the village, two brothers, also succeed in pulling up the spruce tree and pulling off a limb of the old tree. They decide to go out to Sea Lion Rock. Blackskin determines to join them, and when the two brothers try to paddle away without him, he angrily grabs the stern of the canoe and pulls it half out of the water. The brothers agree to allow him on board.

When they get to Sea Lion Rock, the older brother makes his way through the sea lion herd, killing animals, until he reaches the bull sea lion. He catches it by the tail and starts to tear it in half, but the sea lion smashes him with its flipper, injuring him. The same thing happens to the younger brother.

Blackskin then tells the bull sea lion that it was he who pulled up the village tree and pulled off the limb. And he is the nephew of the man the sea lion killed many years ago! He grabs the sea lion by its tail and rips it in half, avenging the death of his uncle.

The second spoon to which I want to draw attention is that pictured in plate 23. Many of my consultants identified one of the images carved on its handle as that of Cannibal, or Gooteel. According to my Tlingit consultants, the Cannibal crest and its story are owned by the G̲aana̲xteidí of the Frog House (X̱íxch'i Hít) at Klukwan. In one well-known version of the story, Cannibal is described as a giant who stands some sixteen feet tall.[64] Whenever the G̲aana̲xteidí Frog House people were drying their salmon, the giant came down from the mountains to devour the catch, and the people starved.

Armed men tried to kill him, but his skin was so thick they could not. Then Cannibal began to prey on people, and soon he had killed and eaten half the tribe.

To protect themselves, the survivors dug a deep pit like the ones hunters used to trap brown bears. They placed a net made of sinew at the bottom of the pit and covered it with pieces of wood to conceal it. The next morning one of the men went to Cannibal's house to lure him out, and Cannibal fell into the trap and was caught in the net. The men piled dry wood on top of him and set it on fire. As the fire burned, Cannibal warned the men that even if nothing remained but his ashes, he would continue to attack and eat them. The men kept the fire burning for four days and nights, until only ashes were left in the pit. But when they stirred the ashes, sparks flew up and changed into mosquitoes that began to bite the men and draw blood. Cannibal's threat had come true.

To stop Cannibal from harassing them, the people carved an image of him holding an emaciated child, half-frog and half-human, in his arms, a representation that honored and appeased the spirit of Cannibal. The carving eventually became a house post in the Frog House at Klukwan, and ever since then members of the Frog House have "fed" the carving by keeping a bowl of hooligan oil in front of it—an unusual practice among the Tlingits.

The human figure on the back of this spoon appears to be carried by Cannibal, who is carved on the front of the handle (see pl. 23). PM 69-30-10/1725. T5106.2. Hillel S. Burger, photographer.

A wolf mask worn at a ceremony in Sitka, Alaska, in 2004. Wolf Houses of the Sitka Kaagwaantaan clan hosted the ceremony commemorating a similar event in Sitka in 1904. Photo by James Poulson, *Daily Sitka Sentinel.*

Spoons Since the Nineteenth Century

Throughout the years when Russia claimed ownership of Alaska, it never completely controlled the Tlingits and Haidas. Much changed in 1867, when the United States purchased the Alaskan territory. The succeeding years brought great social instability and upheaval to Alaska Natives, as we saw from published descriptions of life in Sitka when Edward Fast was collecting there. Protestant missionaries pushed for the assimilation of Alaska Natives, punishing Tlingit and Haida children for speaking their own languages in school, forbidding their attendance at traditional ceremonies such as the _koo.éex'_, and forcibly cutting shamans' long hair, where their power resided and which made them more closely resemble animals. Some crest paraphernalia, including carved horned spoons, was confiscated or destroyed. Most of the spoons we have today—and the best examples of them—were preserved in museum collections; only a few survived among the Northwest Coast people themselves.

Well into the twentieth century, the Tlingits and Haidas continued to lose much of their material culture, traditional customs, and knowledge. Some tribal leaders even

Tlingits feasting at a ceremony in Sitka, 2004. The ceremony commemorated the last large, traditional potlatch in Sitka, held in 1904. Photo by James Poulson, *Daily Sitka Sentinel*.

lost most of their ability to speak their native tongue. At the same time, many people fiercely resisted the loss of their culture, taking their traditions and ceremonies underground to make sure they were preserved. Memorial feasts, in particular, were targets of U.S. government and missionary suppression, but because of their importance, some people continued to hold them clandestinely.

By and large, however, when the government put an end to the potlatches, people stopped carving spoons. Spoons and ladles were companions to ceremonial dishes, and when people stopped using carved dishes, they stopped using the spoons as well. Today only a few carvers have revived and practice the art. It is difficult to obtain the horns of mountain goats and Dall sheep, and most of the other products for which these animals were hunted in the past are no longer used. Artisans still make robes and hats for use in ceremonials, but the carved bowls they make are primarily sold as tourist art. People no longer use spoons in the same contexts even in feasting. When old bowls and spoons are brought out in contemporary ceremonies, it is as *at.óow*, part of the display of clan and crest regalia.

A commemoration ceremony in Sitka, 2004. *At.óow* of the Kaagwaantaan, hosts of the ceremony, are displayed on a table in the foreground. Clan leaders stand in front wearing Chilkat robes decorated with crests. In back, their guests, of the Raven clan, sit behind a table that displays their regalia, including headdresses, Chilkat robes, Raven's Tail robes, spruce hats, staffs, drums, bentwood boxes, and containers. Photo by James Poulson, *Daily Sitka Sentinel.*

Changes in the local economy have also had their effects. Hunting mountain goats and Dall sheep takes time and great skill, and few Tlingits or Haidas now have the necessary time, resources, or skills. Cow horn, although sometimes used for carved spoons, never acquired the same symbolic value as the traditional materials, because it is a domestic material that did not come from the animals and spirits of the high country.

By the 1950s Native peoples on the Northwest Coast were beginning to regain control of their cultures and to restore some of their lost practices and bring them out into the open again. In 1971, the Alaska Native Claims Settlement Act restored millions of acres of Alaska land to Native ownership and dramatically increased Native Alaskans' ability to control their own destinies and recover their lost heritage.

Now, at the beginning of the twenty-first century, Tlingit and Haida culture is strong and growing stronger every year. Memorial feasts and other ceremonials are held openly and with great pride. Ceremonies have been revived, modified, and adapted for new uses. An example was a ceremony held in May 2003 to honor a living elder, the first of its kind. Termed an "honor potlatch," the ceremony celebrated the life and contributions of Tlingit elder Cecilia Kunz (see p. 39). The evening of speeches, dances, gift distribution, and feasting in her honor was structured along the lines of the traditional memorial ceremony, the *koo.éex'*.

Also typical of this resurgence was a commemorative ceremony held in Sitka in October 2004. About four hundred Tlingits and Haidas from throughout Southeast Alaska came together for an event celebrating the centennial of a week-long *koo.éex'* that had been hosted by the three Wolf Houses of the Kaagwaantaan clan in Sitka in December 1904. At the time, the governor of Alaska, John Brady, had described that event as "the last potlatch." Yet a century later, in the same town, the *koo.éex'* was alive and well. A set of old, carved horn spoons that had been handed down within one family, although not used to serve food during the ceremony as it once had been, was displayed in a position of honor on a table directly behind the clan chiefs. Many participants wore traditional regalia. Spoons and regalia alike not only stood as powerful symbols of the rebirth of Tlingit and Haida culture but also spoke eloquently of the Tlingit past. "The family silver of the nobility" still had many important stories to tell.

Color Plates

PLATE 1

Tlingit ceremonial spoon
depicting a sea lion
10-47-10/76830
Alaska, circa 1865–1900
Mountain goat horn
15.3 x 5 x 5 cm*
Collector unknown

THE FIGURE ON THIS ONE-PIECE SPOON appears to represent a sea lion, *taan*, with a body shape showing flippers, backbone, and ribs. Although the face somewhat resembles that of a sea wolf, that mythological creature would more likely have sharp teeth rather than flat ones and is sometimes depicted with gills. A small bird forms the finial of the handle.

A sea lion figures prominently in the tale of Dukt'ootl', a man from the Raven moiety also known as Blackskin and Strong Man, who, after training for many years to improve his self-discipline and gain strength, once tore a large sea lion in half (see pp. 49–50 and pl. 3). According to my consultants, the Kiks.ádi and L'uknax.ádi clans, both of the Raven moiety, claim ownership of the sea lion crest. (Opposite: T4925.1; detail, back of handle: T4924.2. Hillel S. Burger, photographer.)

Drawing of sea lion by Edward Malin from *Totem Poles of the Pacific Northwest Coast*, fig. 66.

*All measurements are given as length x width x depth at widest point.

THE BOWL OF THIS TWO-PIECE SPOON is made of Dall sheep horn, and the handle of mountain goat horn. The bowl is attached to the handle with five copper rivets. The figure at the base of the handle may represent a giant clam, *xéet'*, with its "neck" sticking straight up. A human being kneels against the clam's neck. The design above the kneeling figure is more abstract and could be a bird's head. One expert on Tlingit spoons suggested that the figure at the base might be a hawk rather than a clam. (On totem poles, which are closest to spoons in terms of their carving style, hawks often look like eagles, but their beaks are generally shorter and do not hook down over the lower beak as this one does.)

In 1904, John Swanton recorded the story "The Big Clam," which he later published in his book *Tlingit Myths and Texts*.[65] The story went that at the far end of Tenakee Inlet lay a bay called Where-Sweetness-Killed-a-Person. One summer, when people were there drying salmon, several girls crossed the bay in a canoe and never came back. The people suspected their disappearance had something to do with Big Clam, who lived in Tenakee Inlet below a high cliff. Big Clam always had its valves open, and closed them over any canoe that came near.

Hearing about Big Clam, Raven told a mink to ask the clam to stick its head out of the water so everyone could see it. The clam did so, and the men of the village plunged sharp sticks into it, killing it. The place where this happened came to be called Clam-slide.

According to my Tlingit consultants, the Neix̲.ádi clan at Saxman, along with the Shangukeidí (also know as Dagisdinaa) clan—all of the Eagle moiety—own the Giant Clam crest, *xéet'*. David Katzeek and my other consultants agreed that the story took place in the vicinity of Saxman. (Opposite: T4876.2; right, back of spoon: T5029.2. Hillel S. Burger, photographer.)

69-30-10
1723

PLATE 3
Tlingit ceremonial spoon depicting
a sea lion and Dukt'ootl'
69-30-10/1738
Circa 1840–1865
Mountain goat horn
19.3 X 5.4 X 5.4 cm
Collected by Edward G. Fast,
1867–1868, Alaska

THE FIGURE AT THE BASE of the handle of this one-piece spoon represents a sea lion. The man above the sea lion is the legendary hero Dukt'ootl', also known as Strong Man or Blackskin, who avenges his uncle's death by slaughtering the sea lion who had killed the uncle. On the upper part of the bowl, a small piece of what may have been abalone shell inlay is missing. Tlingit clans that claim to own Dukt'ootl' include the Gaanax.ádi, the Gaanaxteidí, the L'uknax.ádi, and the Taakw.aaneidí, all of the Raven moiety. According to David Katzeek, the Gaanaxteidí have in their possession a house post called the Strong Man Pole (Dukt'ootl'). Such possession, according to Tlingit tradition, is proof of ownership. (Opposite: T4904.1; detail at left: T4905.2. Hillel S. Burger, photographer.)

Drawing of Strong Man by Edward Malin from *Totem Poles of the Pacific Northwest Coast*, fig. 110.

PLATE 4

Tlingit ceremonial spoon
depicting a Thunderbird
69-30-10/1740
Circa 1840–1867
Mountain goat horn
15.5 × 5.5 × 5.5 cm
Collected by Edward G. Fast,
1867–1868, Alaska

THE FIGURE ON THE HANDLE of this one-piece spoon may represent a humanlike Thunderbird, a giant supernatural bird said to cause thunder and lightning. The figure at the apex might be a dogfish.

My consultants told me that the Shangukeidí clan of the Eagle moiety owns the Thunderbird crest, *xeitl*.[66] They live in Klukwan, Yakutat, Kake, and Klawock. In 1949, in Yakutat, Frederica de Laguna recorded Frank Italio explain why all the Shangukeidí belong to the Thunderbird clan.[67] The story tells how some people traveling by canoe went ashore at a place in Yakutat called Glacier Point to have lunch. When they resumed their journey, they left behind a napping four-year-old boy. By the time they noticed him missing, it was too late: to reach Glacier Point again they would have to paddle against the current for four days, and by then he would have died of starvation. They had a big potlatch for the boy, and the Shangukeidí made a mourning song to record the sad event.

When the boy woke up all alone, he started crying. A passing Thunderbird, who looked like a human, heard his cries and took him into a cave, where he raised him. When the boy grew into a young man, he began to miss his family, and the Thunderbird thought it would be best for him to return home. Before he left, the boy grew Thunderbird quills on his lower arms and legs. When he returned home he instructed his people to build a Thunderbird House. He also painted the Thunderbird screen inside the house and composed a song. (House screens are large wooden partitions, carved and painted with crest signs, that face the front door of the house of the clan leader, whose ritual possessions are kept behind it.)

David Katzeek, a Shangukeidí, heard a different story from his grandparents and told it to me in September 2003. Again the event took place on a beach near Yakutat. Two boys were practicing shooting with their bows and arrows. One arrow landed next to a log that looked like a large feather. When they went to fetch their arrows, one boy kicked at the object, saying, "What is this stupid thing?" The object exploded, killing them. One night as their mother was mourning, she had a dream in which a man said, "I am Xeitl [Thunder]. I am the one who took your sons. I am sorry for the grief I have caused you, and so in the place of your children I will give you my song and my crest." He gave her the Thunderbird song and screen, and so her house became the Thunderbird House, Xeitl Hít. (T4957.2. Hillel S. Burger, photographer.)

PLATE 5
Tlingit ceremonial spoon
depicting an eagle
69-30-10/1750
Circa 1840–1865
Mountain goat horn
22.9 × 5 × 4.9 cm
Collected by Edward G. Fast,
1867–1868, Alaska

THE BOWL OF THIS TWO-PIECE SPOON was once affixed to the handle with rivets that are now missing. The two pieces were repaired at some point with two thin copper threads to keep them together.

The figure at the base of the handle resembles a rock. Above it stands what may be an eagle with a salmon in its claws. The eagle seems to be wearing a hat with three rings above it, an emblem of prestige.

According to my consultants, several clans of the Eagle moiety own the Eagle crest, including the Dakl'aweidí, the Kaagwaantaan, the Neix̱.ádi in Saxman, the S'eet'kweidí, the Shangukeidí, the Teikweidí, and the Yanyeidí. The following is my summary of a story about how the Neix̱.ádi acquired the Eagle crest. It is derived from a version Swanton recorded at Wrangell, Alaska, in 1904.[68]

A young Neix̱.ádi man was so poor that he often had no food to eat. One morning, starving as usual, he heard a voice say, "I have come after you." Then he saw a young eagle nearby with an old blanket on its back. The eagle, who looked just like a human being, approached the young man, laid his blanket on the ground, and said, "My grandfather has sent me for you." The man followed the eagle to a house deep in the forest. Everything inside looked exactly as if the house were inhabited by humans. The eagle people fed the man all kinds of delicious food, and eventually he married an eagle.

The man, now transformed into an eagle, learned from his in-laws how to fish and hunt. But back home, his mother and brothers were still starving. Every time he saw one of his brothers desperately trying to get some fish, he left fish and meat on the path back to their home. One night his mother heard a voice saying, "It is I, mother, who provides for you all this fish and meat." The eagle-man then told her where to get food. On one occasion he said he was going camping at a certain place, and she and his brothers should join him there. They did as they were told and soon were busy drying the fish he had caught for them. And one day as they were preparing meat, they saw an eagle perched on a nearby branch. The eagle told his mother that he was her late son, now living with the eagle people. That is why to this day the Neix̱.ádi claim the Eagle crest as theirs. (T4941.2. Hillel S. Burger, photographer.)

PLATE 6

Tlingit ceremonial spoon depicting
human figures, an owl, and frogs
14-27-10/85897
Circa 1840–1880
Mountain goat horn, metal,
abalone shell
23.4 x 6.9 x 5.8 cm
Collected by Lt. George Thornton
Emmons, Dixon Entrance,
British Columbia

FOUR METAL RIVETS AFFIX THE HANDLE of this
two-piece spoon to the bowl. The figure at the base of
the handle represents the face and arms of an upside-
down human being with his eyes wide open. An owl
stands above him, and above the owl is the face of
another inverted human with his eyes closed, which
may suggest a man's spirit. Above the human face are
two eyes, one on either side of the spoon, and above the eyes are three frogs.

Another possibility is that the figure with closed eyes represents a frog in human form.
One can also see in it a creature or a figure of mythology that holds an inverted man in its
mouth. The style and iconography of the creature at the apex resemble those of the dogfish
design on twelve other horn spoons in the Peabody collections. The Dogfish crest is
claimed by the Shangukeidí, of the Eagle moiety. The Kik.sádi in Sitka, members of the
Raven moiety, are the principal owners of the Frog crest, *Xíxch'i,* though other clans also
own it. According to David Katzeek, to have the dogfish (*x'átgu*) associated with any Raven
crest is untraditional. (Opposite: T4947; details: right, T4919.1, below, T5024.2. Hillel S.
Burger, photographer.)

PLATE 7

Tlingit ceremonial spoon depicting
a frog, a human, and a raven
14-27-10/85897.1
Circa 1840–1880
Mountain goat horn, metal
27.5 x 7 x 8 cm
Collected by Lt. George
Thornton Emmons,
Dixon Entrance, British Columbia

THE BOWL OF THIS TWO-PIECE SPOON is fixed to the handle with one metal rivet. The figure at the base of the handle represents a frog; above it, a man leans on the head of the frog. Next we see the characteristic raven's head, with its long beak and spread wings. Above it is an unidentified creature with its tongue reaching down to the raven and two animal ears on the top of its head.

The raven is the main crest animal of all Tlingit Raven clans. For the Tlingits, Raven, or *yéil*, is both benefactor and trickster. In Tlingit and Haida stories, he is always intelligent, always curious, and often mischievous. According to John Swanton, Raven first came to life when he flew to a place near the Nass River where the powerful chief of a big house lived with his family.[69] Raven got the chief's daughter pregnant by turning into a tiny piece of dirt and dropping into a spring from which the family drew water. The young woman drank from the spring, swallowed the dirt, and became pregnant. She then gave birth to Raven in human form.

By the time Raven was grown up, he could change from human to animal and back again. He acquired even more power from his mother's father, who had many sacred bundles hanging on the walls of his house. When Raven asked for a bundle, his kindly grandfather could not refuse him. Raven asked for one bundle after another until his grandfather had at last given him all of them.

Opening the first bundle, Raven created the stars. With the second he gave birth to the moon. From the third he created daylight. As he opened the last bundle, he made the cry of a raven and flew up through the smoke hole. He then flew to a man who had a precious spring, swallowed it, and created rivers and salmon streams. He created land, mountains, plants, sea creatures, birds, and trees. The living creatures and even the inanimate objects he created, such as rocks, could transform themselves into other beings. That was how the Tlingit people came into the world Raven created for them.

In 1980, Austin Hammond, a Tlingit elder and a leader of the Raven moiety, said during a speech, "It was Raven who showed us how to get our food. Raven knew what was good for us and taught us how to live. Raven exists in our legends and in our lives."[70] (Opposite: T4917.2; detail: T4918.2. Hillel S. Burger, photographer.)

PLATE 8

Tlingit ceremonial spoon depicting a
frog, a hawk, and possibly a dragonfly
69-30-10/1726
Circa 1840–1865
Mountain goat horn,
Dall sheep horn, copper, metal
22.5 x 6 x 5.3 cm
Collected by Edward G. Fast,
1867–1868, Alaska

THE BOWL OF THIS TWO-PIECE SPOON is made of Dall sheep horn, and the handle of mountain goat horn. The bowl is fixed to the handle with five original copper rivets; three lead rivets appear to have been added later.

The figure at the base of the handle is probably a frog. Above it is a hawk, also called the golden eagle. The figure at the apex might represent a bird with a short, pointed beak and a tail. Several of my consultants, however, strongly suggested that this figure with paired wings could represent a dragonfly, *kaashaashxáat'*.

In December 2002, Leonard John, a member of the Deisheetaan clan from Angoon (Xootsnoowú), on Admiralty Island, told me a story about an event that happened there. Two brothers who were out hunting decided to rest and soon fell asleep. Meanwhile, out on the bay, a pod of killer whales started to fight. A dragonfly landed on the forehead of one of the brothers and woke him up just in time for him to witness the fight. Johnny Marks, a Tlingit elder, told me that the Deisheetaan from Angoon acquired the Dragonfly crest as a war payment.

Similarly, according to an account given by Sergei Kan, the Deisheetaan may have obtained the Frog crest from the L'uknax.ádi clan in payment for a man's death. The L'uknax.ádi have a Frog House, Xíxch'i Hít, in Sitka.[71] (Opposite: T5043.2; detail: T4887.2. Hillel S. Burger, photographer.)

Drawing of frog by Jim Gilbert,
courtesy Raven Publishing Inc.

PLATE 9

Tlingit ceremonial spoon
depicting a frog, a hawk,
and a squatting human
69-30-10/1728
Circa 1840–1867
Mountain goat horn,
abalone shell, copper
21 x 5.3 x 5.4 cm
Collected by Edward G. Fast,
1867–1868, Alaska

THE BOWL OF THIS TWO-PIECE SPOON is affixed to the handle with five copper rivets. The figure at the base of the handle is a frog, above which stands a humanoid hawk. The eyes of both figures are inlaid with abalone shell. Above the hawk is an inverted face that could be a hawk in human form, a human being, or an ancestor. The feet and hands on the back of the spoon belong to that being.

Finally, there is a squatting human with his tongue connected to the figure below. Steve Henrickson told me in 2005 that the motif of the shared tongue "is generally considered symbolic of the passing of power and knowledge" or of communication. The figure holds his tongue with his right hand, and with his left, something on top of his head, perhaps a raven's beak represented on a hat.

According to David Katzeek, this design depicts the story of Hawk. The hawk was known to prey on human beings, but Raven intervened and made the hawk eat human excrement. From then on the hawk never preyed on humans. (Opposite: T4889.1; detail, back of handle: T4890.2. Hillel S. Burger, photographer.)

Drawing of hawk by Edward Malin
from *Totem Poles of the Pacific
Northwest Coast*, fig. 72.

PLATE 10

Tlingit ceremonial spoon depicting a
frog, human faces, and a dragonfly
69-30-10/1731
Circa 1840–1867
Mountain goat horn, copper
23 x 5.4 x 7.3 cm
Collected by Edward G. Fast,
1867–1868, Alaska

BOTH THE BOWL AND HANDLE of this spoon are made of
mountain goat horn. A patch of copper is wrapped around the upper
part of the bowl to reinforce the fastening of the bowl and handle.
There is one rivet at the base of the handle.

The figure at the base of the handle is a frog. Above it are two back-
to-back human faces. The carving above the human faces represents a dragonfly;
note its wings and its head at the apex. (Opposite: T4899.2; details: left, front of
handle, T4890.2; right, back of handle, T4953.2. Hillel S. Burger, photographer.)

Drawing of dragonfly by Edward
Malin from *Totem Poles of the Pacific
Northwest Coast*, fig. 74A.

PLATE 11
Tlingit or Haida ceremonial spoon
depicting a frog and a sculpin
69-30-10/1742
Circa 1840–1865
Mountain goat horn
15.1 x 5.5 x 6.1 cm
Collected by Edward G. Fast,
1867–1868, Alaska

Tlingit or Haida ceremonial
or shaman spoon or ladle depicting
a war helmet and an octopus
45-28-10/27704
Circa 1840–1865
Mountain goat horn, Dall sheep
horn, copper
40 x 9.5 x 8 cm
Collected by Dr. Samuel Cabot,
Prince of Wales Island, Alaska

THE FIGURE ON THE UPPER PART of the bowl of spoon 69-30-10/1742, shown in two views on this page, represents a frog. The whole handle of this one-piece spoon is a sculpin. The upper part of the bowl near the handle might once have been decorated with a tiny piece of abalone shell. The sculpin, or bullhead, was sacred to shamans. This sculpin's large, staring eyes suggest Haida manufacture, as they do on the spoon in plate 24. The frog in the sculpin's mouth is typical of many Haida carvings in which beings are eating, being eaten, or extruding other beings in continuous, interlocking patterns. Haidas of the Eagle clan own the Sculpin and Frog crests.

The bowl of the two-piece spoon or ladle opposite (45-28-10/27704) is made of Dall sheep horn, and the handle, with its abalone shell inlays, is of mountain goat horn. The bowl is attached to the handle with two copper rivets. The figure at the base of the handle resembles a war helmet, which could indicate its power to protect its owner in battle and on dangerous journeys to the spirit world. The eyes on the helmet were probably once decorated with abalone shell inlays. Above the helmet is the head of an octopus, identifiable by its sharp beak, and above that is a single tentacle. The octopus is a Haida crest, and the figures' large, prominent eyes and the uncarved back of the handle also suggest Haida manufacture. Tlingit spoons and totem poles tend to be developed from all sides.

Very large, decorated feast ladles like the one opposite were probably *at.óow* and were used both for serving food and during eating contests at potlatches. The competition to eat the greatest quantity of food in the shortest amount of time was a display of individual strength and power. If this was a shaman's spoon, however, it would have been used exclusively by its owner and not in feasting competitions. Both Tlingits and Haidas often associate the octopus with shamanism. Among the Haidas it was also a crest of the Raven moiety. (Opposite: T5109.1. Above, T4944.2; right, T4940.2. Hillel S. Burger, photographer.)

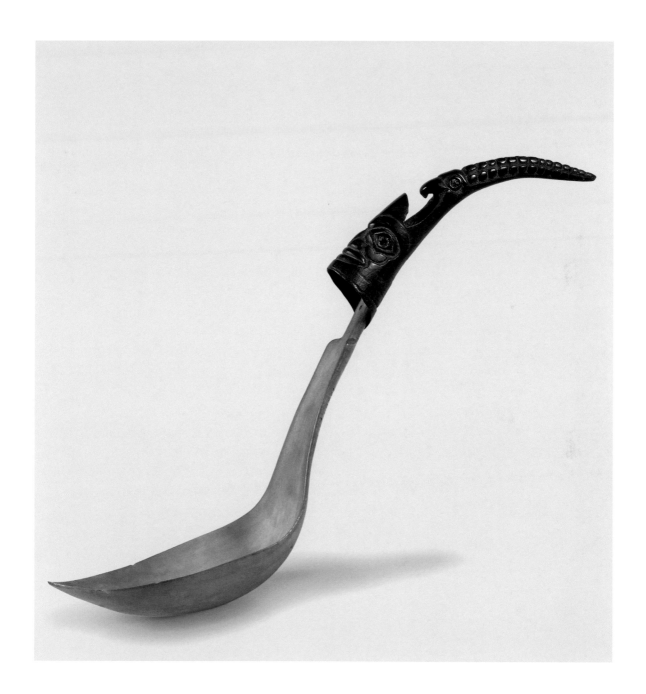

PLATE 12
Tlingit ceremonial spoon depicting
an owl and a man wearing a hat
69-30-10/1749
Circa 1840–1865
Mountain goat horn,
abalone shell, copper
20.7 x 5.5 x 5.2 cm
Collected by Edward G. Fast,
1867–1868, Alaska

THE RIVETS THAT ONCE FASTENED the bowl and handle of this two-piece spoon together are missing. The pieces are now attached to each other with a copper thread.

The figure at the base of the handle is perhaps a frog or a sculpin's head with abalone shell inlays in its eyes. Above it is an owl with a human body. At the apex is a man wearing a hat ornamented with basketry cylinders. These rings, status objects that were added to hats, may represent a potlatch given by the chief or, according to Steve Henrickson, the number of slaves killed at a potlatch. David Katzeek believes the man at the apex is holding some kind of object or animal, perhaps a halibut, in his mouth.

Katzeek, however, says the middle figure depicts a hawk rather than an owl. He related the following story in relation to this spoon: Hawk had a long, beautiful beak that Raven envied. One day Raven sent Hawk to get fire from an island where fire erupted from a mountain. Raven wanted to cook the salmon he had tricked into coming on shore. While getting the fire, Hawk burned off his beak, and Raven no longer had to be envious. That is why the beaks of hawks are short and rounded.

The story was told to Katzeek by the late James Klanott, Tlingit historian of the Raven House in Haines, and by the late Marie White-Klanoth-Kasko, Tlingit historian of the Thunderbird House in Klukwan. (Opposite: T4912.2; detail: T4911.2. Hillel S. Burger, photographer.)

Drawing of sculpin by Edward
Malin from *Totem Poles of the Pacific
Northwest Coast*, fig. 70.

Tlingit ceremonial spoon
depicting human faces and a frog
69-30-10/1757
Circa 1840–1865
Mountain goat horn
17.8 x 5.6 x 6.4 cm
Collected by Edward G. Fast,
1867–1868

AT THE BASE OF THE HANDLE of this one-piece spoon is an inverted human face. The next figure is probably another human face with its mouth wide open. The figure in the middle of the handle is probably a frog, and above it is a creature with a human face squatting with its arms stretched out on either side of the frog's head. Its hands extend to the top of the head of the creature with its mouth open. On the back of the handle one can see a pair of human legs, and above that the feet and calves of the squatting figure.

David Katzeek interpreted these figures as telling the story of how the Kiks.ádi clan of the Raven moiety acquired the Frog crest. To summarize the story as recorded by Swanton,[72] a man and his wife were crossing the mouth of a big bay in a canoe when it became so foggy that they could not see even the water around them. As they sat waiting for the fog to lift, they suddenly heard a voice singing, "We picked up a man; you picked up a man. They captured a man; they captured a man; you've captured a man." The powerful voice echoed among the mountains.

The fog now started to lift, and the voice grew increasingly nearer. Finally the couple saw a little frog nearby. The man said, "This frog is going to be mine, and I am going to claim it." The woman said, "No, this frog is mine, and I am the one who is going to claim it." They quarreled for a while, but finally the husband let his wife have the frog. She took it ashore, treating it like a child. She carried the frog up to the woods and put it down by a lake. From that time forward her people were Kiks.ádi and claimed the frog as a crest. (Opposite: T5113.1; detail: T4945.1. Hillel S. Burger, photographer.)

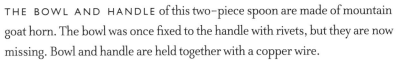

PLATE 14

Tlingit ceremonial spoon depicting
Gunakadeit, the sea monster
69-30-10/1732
Circa 1840–1865
Mountain goat horn,
abalone shell, copper
26.5 x 6.5 x 6.8 cm
Collected by Edward G. Fast,
1867–1868, Alaska

THE BOWL AND HANDLE of this two-piece spoon are made of mountain goat horn. The bowl was once fixed to the handle with rivets, but they are now missing. Bowl and handle are held together with a copper wire.

The figure at the base of the handle, with abalone shell inlays, represents a rock. Sitting on the rock is what most of my consultants identified as Gunakadeit, a sea monster, recognizable by the gills carved on the side of its mouth. Gunakadeit is holding a halibut. Above the sea monster is a bear, and above the bear's head is a creature that could be a dogfish. One of my consultants suggested that it might be an insect. The eyes of the creature at the apex used to be decorated with what probably were abalone shell inlays.

John Swanton recorded one version of a story about Gunakadeit.[73] A young man from a noble family married a girl from another high-ranking clan. The man's mother-in-law disliked him, calling him lazy and worthless. Tired of being insulted, the man decided to prove his mother-in-law wrong.

One day he went to a lake where a powerful sea monster lived, because he knew that if one looked at a sea monster, one would become lucky and wealthy. He trapped the sea monster, skinned it, and put on its skin. Soon he discovered that he could swim underwater and was as powerful as the sea monster. He was able to bring home enough food—salmon, halibut, seals, and sea lions—for the entire village. But he could hunt only at night. If he was not home before dawn, he would lose his power and his life.

One night he failed to make it home before dawn. His wife repeatedly went down to the beach at night and called for him. Before long the sea monster appeared and told her to climb onto his back. She did so, and they swam down to his house, where they and their children have lived ever since. To this day, if one sees Gunakadeit, one will have great luck and acquire great wealth.

Clans of both the Eagle and Raven moieties own the sea monster story. Tlingit clans that are said to own the Sea Monster crest include, from the Eagle moiety, the Naanyaa.aayí in Wrangell and, from the Raven moiety, the Gaanax.ádi in Klawock, the Gaanaxteidí in Klukwan, and the T'akdeintaan in Hoonah. (Opposite: T4942.1; detail: T4946.2. Hillel S. Burger, photographer.)

PLATE 15

Tlingit ceremonial spoon depicting
G̲unakadeit, the sea monster
14-27-10/85897.3
Circa 1840–1880
Mountain goat horn, metal
25.9 x 5.5 x 8.8 cm
Collected by Lt. George Thornton
Emmons, Dixon Entrance,
British Columbia

THE BOWL OF THIS TWO-PIECE spoon is attached to the handle with two horn rivets. The figure at the base of the handle probably represents the sea monster G̲unakadeit, also sometimes called K̲ooligi, a name that refers to something mysterious, awesome, astounding, and humbling—a power greater than oneself. According to David Katzeek, G̲unakadeit holds the inverted head of a human in its mouth. The reason for identifying this figure as the sea monster is that it has long ears in the shape of dorsal fins. A bear would have shorter ears. Above the ears are probably the joints, then the sea monster's pectoral fins. Above them is the joint of the tail, and then the tail or flippers. (Opposite: T4929.2; detail: T4930.2. Hillel S. Burger, photographer.)

Drawing of sea monster by Jim Gilbert,
courtesy Raven Publishing Inc.

PLATE 16

Tlingit ceremonial spoon depicting
Gunakadeit and a whale
14-27-10/85897.2
Circa 1840–1880
Mountain goat horn, metal, copper
23 x 5.7 x 6.3 cm
Collected by Lt. George Thornton
Emmons, Dixon Entrance,
British Columbia

TWO COPPER RIVETS attach the bowl of this
two-piece spoon to the handle. The figure at the
base of the handle probably represents Gunakadeit,
the sea monster, holding a seal in his hands. Above
Gunakadeit is the inverted head of a creature that
looks human, with its arms and hands embedded
in Gunakadeit's ears. Resting inside his chest are the head, pectoral fins, and flukes of
a whale. The tongue of the human creature is connected with the mouth of the whale.
Above the fluke stands a creature with a humanlike body. Looking at the spoon from
the side, one can see at the apex a bird's head resembling that of a raven. At the back
of the spoon, the feet of the human being are visible.

In the story of Gunakadeit recounted in connection with plate 14, the whale is the
last animal he brings to his village after he kills and becomes the sea monster. David
Katzeek explained that after fighting the whale, the man was so exhausted that he
could not leave the spirit of Gunakadeit before dawn, and so he died. (Opposite:
T4931.2; right, T4933.3. Hillel S. Burger, photographer.)

Drawing of whale by Edward Malin
from *Totem Poles of the Pacific
Northwest Coast*, fig. 63.

PLATE 17

Tlingit ceremonial spoon
depicting a raven
69-30-10/1737
Circa 1840–1865
Mountain goat horn
16 × 5 × 5.7 cm
Collected by Edward G. Fast,
1867–1868, Alaska

THE FIGURE ON THIS ONE-PIECE SPOON probably represents a raven, although it could be a loon. One tiny piece of what was probably abalone shell inlay in the upper center part of the bowl, near the handle, is now missing.

The design on the handle might represent Raven when he dived into the ocean inside the stomach of a whale (see pl. 18 for the whole story). It might also refer to another story of the Raven cycle, about the time he created a woman who lived under the earth and was in charge of the tides. One day Raven decided to explore the ocean. He asked the woman to raise the water level so that he could dive in and start to survey underwater.[74]

If the bird on the handle is indeed a raven, then the spoon could belong to any of the Raven clans, because all Tlingits from the Raven moiety can use the Raven as a crest. As a Gaanax.ádi, Raven is of particular importance to the members of that clan. Use of the Raven design, however, is not restricted to the Raven clans. People in the Eagle moiety, for example, although they cannot display the Raven as a crest, may use the Raven design as a symbol of power or protection on items such as amulets and shamans' rattles. Despite being a notorious trickster, Raven was a benefactor to all Tlingit people.[75] (Opposite: T4903; detail: T4902.1. Hillel S. Burger, photographer.)

Drawing of Raven by Jim Gilbert,
courtesy Raven Publishing Inc.

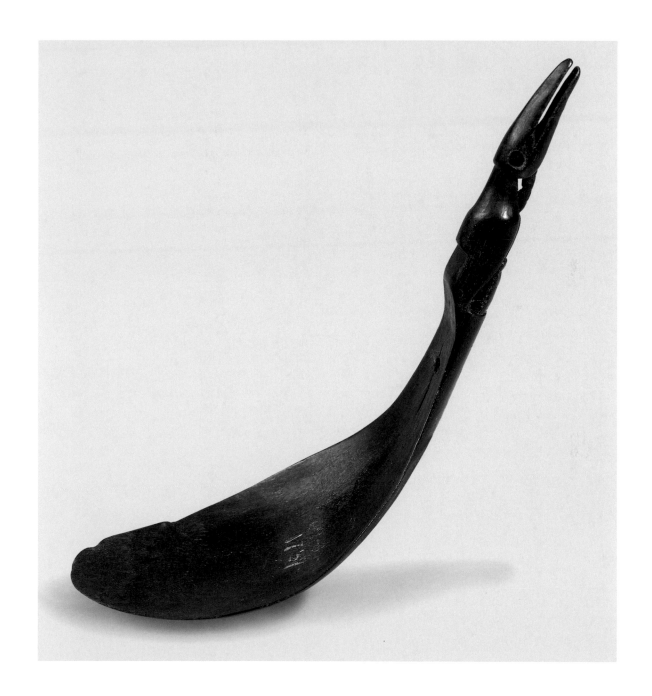

THE BOWL OF THIS TWO-PIECE SPOON is made of Dall sheep horn, and the handle, with abalone shell inlays, of mountain goat horn. The bowl is fastened to the handle with one metal rivet. The figure at the base of the handle looks something like a sea lion, but because it lacks ears, it probably was meant to depict a whale. The back of the whale is filled with the carving of a raven, with abalone shell in its eyes.[76]

Viola Garfield recorded a version of a Tlingit story called "Raven and the Whale."[76] In it, Raven spots a whale in the ocean one day and decides to kill it. He flies over the whale and enters its mouth. Once inside the whale's body, he starts a fire to cook all the fish the animal has swallowed. When Raven runs out of fish, he begins cutting fat from the whale's body. Soon the whale dies, and Raven finds himself trapped inside.

Then Raven begins singing, "I wish the whale would drift to a good sandy beach, I wish for a fine sandy beach." As he sings, the whale's body lands on a beach near a village. When several young men approach it, they hear a song: "I wish there was a man strong enough to cut open the whale." The frightened young men dash back to the village to tell everyone, and several strong, mature men go to the beach to butcher the whale. Raven is saved, but he flies out covered with grease.

Back in the village, the people make a song about the greasy creature that flew from the whale's stomach. Raven is ashamed and never comes back, so the humans get to eat the meat that was supposed to be his.

In another version, Raven returns to the village in human form and tells the villagers that it would be dangerous to eat the flesh of a whale with a human voice. The men agree and soon leave. Raven then eats the meat of the whale. (Opposite: T5107.1; details: front of handle, left, T5108.1, back of handle, right, T5114.1. Hillel S. Burger, photographer.)

PLATE 19
Tlingit ceremonial spoon
depicting the hunter Kaats'
69-30-10/1724
Circa 1840–1867
Mountain goat horn,
Dall sheep horn, copper
22 x 5.8 x 6 cm
Collected by Edward G. Fast,
1867–1868, Alaska

MOUNTAIN GOAT HORN FORMS THE HANDLE of this two-piece spoon. The bowl, made of Dall sheep horn, is fixed to the handle with five copper rivets and reinforced by a patch of copper on the back. According to my consultants, the broken figure at the base of the handle might represent a personified Earth, with eyes that were once inlaid with abalone shell. The man standing above it is probably Kaats', and the two cubs nestled on his chest and abdomen are his children. The figure above the hunter's head resembles a dogfish.

Scholars have recorded a number of versions of the Kaats' story. One, told to Nora Marks Dauenhauer in October 1972,[77] described how Kaats', while out hunting brown bears near Ketchikan, was captured by a female bear. She pulled him into her den, concealed him, and then married him. When she and the other bears took off their skin coats, they looked just like people, and their den looked like a house. Kaats's brothers searched for him but found only his footprints alongside bear tracks. When the youngest brother went into the forest to search with Kaats's dogs, however, they started sniffing the entrance to a den. Kaats' immediately recognized his dogs and greeted his younger brother, but asked him to tell no one that he was living in a den and had children with a bear.

One day, before Kaats' went seal hunting, his bear wife warned him not to speak with his human wife, and he agreed. When they met by a stream, his human wife made fun of his bear children, the "tiny faces with hair on them." Forgetting his promise, he reprimanded his human wife. Years later, when his bear children were grown, they killed Kaats' while he was out hunting. A villager saw the bear wife standing by her dead husband, singing the sacred cry song known as the Brown Bear Song, which several clans still sing to this day. This story illustrates the delicate relationship between animals and humans, between whom Kaats' was a mediator. His wife broke a taboo by insulting bears, however, and Kaats' broke his agreement with his bear wife. For both transgressions, Kaats' had to be killed by his bear children. Because Kaats' gave his life, the Teikweidí acquired the bear as their primary crest. My consultants say the story of Kaats' is also owned by the Kaagwaantaan, Chookaneidí, and Shangukeidí clans of the Eagle moiety. (Opposite: T4877.1; detail of bear child: T4881.1. Hillel S. Burger, photographer.)

PLATE 20
Tlingit ceremonial spoon
depicting bears
69-30-10/1730
Circa 1840–1865
Mountain goat horn, copper, metal
24.6 x 5.6 x 6 cm
Collected by Edward G. Fast,
1867–1868, Alaska

THE BOWL AND HANDLE of this two-piece spoon are made of mountain goat horn. The bowl is affixed to the handle with a metal rivet and a piece of copper.

The figure at the base of the handle represents an island, a reef, or a rock. Squatting on the rock is a bear holding a halibut in its paws, and above it is the face of another bear, perhaps a cub. Next is a figure that my consultants identified variously as a mountain, an eagle, and a raven. One story in the Raven cycle of legends recorded by Swanton suggests that the figure is most likely a raven, because in the story Raven, the powerful trickster, uses clever tactics to outsmart a male bear during a fishing trip.[78]

The story goes that one day, while fishing with Cormorant, Raven caught many halibut, but Bear caught none. He asked Raven what kind of bait he was using. "I use my testicles," he told Bear. Bear at first refused to use his own testicles as bait, but after Raven warned that his wife would be disappointed if he came back empty-handed, he did as Raven directed. Falling into the water, Bear bled to death.

Raven and Cormorant towed Bear's dead body back to shore. Raven then went to the house of Bear's wife and suggested that he roast the halibuts' stomachs for her. On the beach, he cooked the stomachs and then filled them with hot rocks. Then he invited Bear's wife to eat one of them, adding that she should swallow the stomach without chewing it. She swallowed all the food and started to feel sick. Raven brought her some water, and when she drank it, the food in her stomach began to boil. Soon she was dead, and Raven ate the two bears.

Clans said to own the Bear and Halibut crests include the Neix̱.ádi, of the Eagle moiety, at Saxman, who have a Halibut House, Cháatl Hít. The Teik̲weidí, Kaagwaantaan, and Naanyaa.aayí clans also claim the bear as a crest animal. (Opposite: T4896.1; right: T4895.1. Hillel S. Burger, photographer.)

97

PLATE 21

Tlingit ceremonial spoon
depicting a bear and a loon
973-24-10/52232
Circa 1840–1885
Mountain goat horn,
Dall sheep horn,
abalone shell, copper
28.6 x 6 x 7.2 cm
Collected by Eliot Elisofen,
1940–1972, Alaska

THE BOWL OF THIS TWO-PIECE SPOON is made of Dall sheep horn, and the handle of mountain goat horn. The bowl is affixed to the handle with three copper rivets.

The figure depicted at the base of the handle could be either a rock or a hunter with eyes inlaid with abalone shell. The design immediately above it suggested to Steve Henrickson a bear, because of its ∪-shaped ears and its squatting position. Its eyes, too, are inlaid with abalone shell. The figure at the handle's apex is probably a loon, decorated on both sides with inlaid abalone shell.

The Tlingits occasionally featured loons on sculptures, including totem poles, and in stories. A pole now standing at Saxman, for example—a reproduction of an old pole that once stood at Cape Fox—portrays the adventures of Kaats', the hunter. At the top stands a loon with outstretched wings, symbolizing the experiences of the ancestors of Kaats' before Raven brought daylight to the world. In that story, some Tlingit people were canoeing on Behm Canal, in Saxman territory, when they became lost and could not find their way to open water. Suddenly they heard the call of a loon and followed it until they found daylight at the entrance of the bay.[79]

A loon with wings outstretched also stood at the top of a pole called Bear-in-the-Den that was once housed at the Peabody Museum. In July 2001 the pole was repatriated under the Native American Graves Protection and Repatriation Act (NAGPRA) to the Teikweidí clan in Saxman. (Opposite: T4934.2; detail: T4936.1. Hillel S. Burger, photographer.)

PLATE 22

Tlingit ceremonial spoon
depicting a man wearing a
G̲aangóosh (bear) headdress
69-30-10/1727
Circa 1840–1865
Mountain goat horn,
Dall sheep horn, copper
21.5 x 6 x 2.8 cm
Collected by Edward G. Fast,
1867–1868, Alaska

THE BOWL OF THIS TWO-PIECE SPOON is made of Dall sheep horn, and the handle of mountain goat horn. The bowl is affixed to the handle with two copper rivets.

The figure at the base of the handle is probably an eagle, although several of my consultants thought it could be a wolf. Above its head sits a man wearing a headdress with bear ears; the headdress is named G̲aangóosh. The man's tongue extends from his mouth to another creature that he holds in his arms. Because of the creature's thick lips and long tail, several of my consultants identified it as a land otter.

According to Harold Jacobs, Joe White, Willie Lee, and Charlie Joseph all wore G̲angóosh at the dedication of the Thunderbird House in Klukwan around 1970, demonstrating their clans' ownership of the symbol. White and Lee are Shangukeidí clan members, and Joseph is Kaagwaantaan.

A story published by Ronald L. Olson in 1967 describes the origin of the Bear crest of the Kaagwaantaan clan.[80] Briefly summarized, it tells how Kaagwaantaan people used to catch herring and harvest herring eggs in Neva Strait, near Sitka. One night a large bear stole all the herring eggs that an old widow had drying. The next day she hung more eggs out to dry, but again they were stolen. The woman, now quite upset, called whoever had stolen her food a thief. The bear then killed her and several other people.

The men of the village tried to kill the bear but failed, so they went to Sitka and told their story. All the Kaagwaantaan then decided to hunt the bear. One young man managed to stab it from behind, but as he did so, he fell over backward. As the bear prepared to jump on him, he raised his spear, and when the bear landed, it impaled itself. Another man came to rescue the young man still on the ground, and together they skinned the bear, cut off its ears, and took its teeth and claws. (Opposite: T4872.2; detail: T4873.2. Hillel S. Burger, photographer.)

Mark Jacobs Jr. and his son, Harold Jacobs,
at the Tlingit and Haida Central Council,
Juneau, Alaska, December 2002. Anne-Marie
Victor-Howe, photographer.

PLATE 23
Tlingit ceremonial spoon
depicting Gooteel (Cannibal)
69-30-10/1725
Circa 1840–1865
Mountain goat horn,
Dall sheep horn, metal
23.9 x 6.3 x 7 cm
Collected by Edward G. Fast,
1867–1868, Alaska

THE BOWL OF THIS TWO-PIECE SPOON is made of Dall sheep horn, and the handle of mountain goat horn. The bowl is fixed to the handle with seven metal rivets.

The figures on the spoon's handle are complex. On the front of the handle, the figure at the base might be a personified rock. According to several experts on traditional Tlingit carving, the sheer bulk of the figure suggests that it might be a war helmet, or *shaadaa*. These thick, massive helmets, once worn by Tlingit warriors of high rank, were often carved with the faces of their ancestors. The human head carved on the back of the handle might therefore be either that of the man wearing the armor or the spirit of his deceased ancestor (see p. 51).

The figure above the rock or helmet could be Cannibal, Gooteel, who appears to be carrying a human on his back. Looking at the side of the spoon one can see a strap attached to what could be a carrying board. The strap is bound around Gooteel's chest. Above Cannibal is a human form. Steve Henrickson has suggested, alternatively, that the figure I interpret as Gooteel could be someone carrying a load using a chest tumpline. (Opposite: T4884.1. Hillel S. Burger, photographer.)

PLATE 24

Tlingit ceremonial or shaman
spoon depicting a land otter
69-30-10/1745
Circa 1840–1865
Mountain goat horn
19 x 4.3 x 3.8 cm
Collected by Edward G. Fast,
1867–1868, Alaska

THE FIGURE AT THE BASE OF THE HANDLE of this one-piece spoon is a land otter with his ribs depicted. The artist carved the tongue protruding from the otter's mouth to emphasize its significance as a source of power for the shaman. Above the otter stands a raven.

In most Tlingit stories, land otters are harmful, sometimes terrifying creatures. Yet land otters were the crests of four Tlingit clans, and some stories portray them as kind and helpful to humans. In a story recorded by Frederica de Laguna, a woman who was home alone with her children heard something at the door.[81] A land otter stood there. The woman was so afraid that she fainted, but when at last she recovered her senses, she saw a beautiful young woman by the fire, with thick, light-colored hair. She asked the woman land otter to wish her luck and not to hurt her or her children. "After all," she said, "you are a woman just like me." She fainted again, but this time when she woke up she held a bunch of hair in her hand. It was the hair of the land otter, and it became her amulet.

In 2002, Cecilia Kunz told me another story about a benevolent otter. Some people at their summer camp were being bothered by Land Otter, who threw pinecones against their door and hung their canoe upside down in a tree. The head of the family asked him to stop: "Instead of hurting us, why don't you try to help us get some food?" Land Otter was not seen again for a few days, but then a stranger came to the door. By the shape and thickness of his lips, the family recognized him as Land Otter disguised as a human. They invited him in, but inside the house Land Otter stepped on something sharp and cut his foot. The headman treated the cut with medicine made from a medicinal forest plant. Later, when Land Otter was cured, he expressed his gratitude by bringing halibut and seal meat to the cabin. (Opposite: T5117.1. Hillel S. Burger, photographer.)

105

PLATE 25
Tlingit shaman spoon
depicting a shaman, a land otter,
and an octopus
69-30-10/1729
Circa 1840–1865
Mountain goat horn, copper
26 x 6.3 x 5.1 cm
Collected by Edward G. Fast,
1867–1868, Alaska

BOTH BOWL AND HANDLE of this two-piece spoon, once owned by a shaman who used it as an eating implement, are made of mountain goat horn. Two pegs of mountain goat horn fix the handle to the bowl. They are reinforced by a patch of copper wrapped around the joint.

The eye at the base of the handle represents a personified rock, island, or reef. On it stands a shaman wearing a typical shaman's headdress crowned with mountain goat horns. He holds a land otter's tail in his hands and mouth. He appears to be eating a split land otter that has an exposed ribcage.

On the front and side of the handle at its apex appears the head of an octopus. At the base of the head hang the octopus's human arms, which are abruptly transformed into tentacles with large suckers. On the back of the handle one can see the legs and feet of this human-octopus being. The small creature above the shaman's head is probably the octopus in human form. (Opposite: T4892.2; detail: T5031.2. Hillel S. Burger, photographer.)

Notes

1. See, for example, George F. MacDonald, *Haida Monumental Art: Villages of the Queen Charlotte Islands* (Vancouver: University of British Columbia Press, 1983; reprint, Seattle: University of Washington Press, 1994); George F. MacDonald, *Haida Art* (Seattle: University of Washington Press, 1996); and Peter Macnair, Robert Joseph, and Bruce Greenville, *Down from the Shimmering Sky: Masks of the Northwest Coast* (Seattle: University of Washington Press, 1998).

2. For the spelling of these and other Tlingit words, I received advice from Harold Jacobs and Yarrow Vaara, and also consulted the *English–Tlingit Dictionary: Nouns,* by Henry Davis (Sitka, Alaska: Sheldon Jackson College, 1996 reprint of second edition [1993]; first published 1976).

3. All information attributed to David Katzeek was given to me during interviews in 2002 and 2003.

4. Bill Holm, *Box of Daylight: Northwest Coast Indian Art* (Seattle: Seattle Art Museum and University of Washington Press, 1983), 85. Holm is also the author of *Soft Gold*

(Portland: Oregon Historical Society Press, 1989), the most extensive publication on the Peabody Museum's Northwest Coast collections to date.

5. Frederica de Laguna, "Tlingit," in *Handbook of North American Indians*, vol. 7, *Northwest Coast*, edited by Wayne Suttles (Washington, D.C.: Smithsonian Institution, 1990), 213.

6. See Steven C. Brown, *Native Visions: Evolution in Northwest Coast Art from the Eighteenth Through the Twentieth Century* (Seattle and London: The Seattle Art Museum and the University of Washington Press, 1998, 74ff.; Bill Holm, *Spirit and Ancestor: A Century of Northwest Coast Indian Art at the Burke Museum* (Seattle: Burke Museum and University of Washington Press, 1987), 16.

7. Steve Henrickson, personal communication, 2005. All subsequent unattributed references to information provided by Henrickson are from this written communication.

8. Holm, *Box of Daylight*, 163.

9. Laurence C. Thompson and M. Dale Kinkade, "Languages," in *Handbook of North American Indians*, vol. 7, *Northwest Coast*, edited by Wayne Suttles (Washington, D.C.: Smithsonian Institution Press, 1990), 31.

10. Holm, *Spirit and Ancestor,* 182.

11. George Thornton Emmons, *The Tlingit Indians* (Seattle: University of Washington Press, 1991), 132.

12. Emil Teichmann, *A Journey to Alaska in the Year 1868: Being a Diary of the Late Emil Teichmann,* edited by Oscar Teichmann (New York: Argosy—Antiquarian, 1963 [1925]), 208.

13. Information and quotations in this and the next two paragraphs are drawn from Teichmann, *Journey to Alaska,* 9, 174, 185–187, 189, 190, 209.

14. Steve Henrikson, "Alaska Native Art Displayed by Early Alaskan Museums," paper presented at the annual meeting of the Native American Art Studies Association, Portland, Oregon, October 24–27, 2001.

15. The discussion of Fast's collecting methods is drawn from Teichmann, *Journey to Alaska,* 194, 210–213.

16. This letter is quoted in Frederica de Laguna, "George Thornton Emmons as Ethnographer," in Emmons, *Tlingit Indians*, xvii.

17. This letter is quoted in Jean Low, "Lieutenant George Thornton Emmons, USN, 1852–1945," in Emmons, *Tlingit Indians*, xxviii.

18. Quoted in Low, "Lieutenant Emmons," xxix.

19. De Laguna, "Emmons as Ethnographer," xviii.

20. Jean Baudrillard, "The System of Collecting," in *The Culture of Collecting*, edited by John Elsner and Roger Cardinal (Cambridge, Mass.: Harvard University Press, 1994), 7.

21. Information about Emmons in the remainder of this section is drawn from Jean Low, "Lieutenant Emmons," xxvii–xl.

22. Nora Marks Dauenhauer and Richard Dauenhauer, eds., *Haa Ḵusteeyí, Our Culture: Tlingit Life Stories* (Seattle: University of Washington Press; Juneau: Sealaska Heritage Foundation, 1994), 15.

23. Sergei Kan, *Symbolic Immortality: The Tlingit Potlatch of the Nineteenth Century* (Washington, D.C.: Smithsonian Institution Press, 1989), 69.

24. Dauenhauer and Dauenhauer, *Haa Ḵusteeyí*, 16; de Laguna, "Tlingit," 213.

25. Dauenhauer and Dauenhauer, *Haa Ḵusteeyí,* 17.

26. Erna Gunther, *Art in the Life of the Northwest Coast Indians* (Portland, Ore.: Portland Art Museum, 1966), 27.

27. De Laguna, "Tlingit," 213.

28. Rosita Worl, "Tlingit *At.óow*: Tangible and Intangible Property," Ph.D. dissertation, Department of Anthropology, Harvard University, Cambridge, Mass., 1998, 114. Written by a Tlingit fluent in her native language, this dissertation explores the fundamental concept of *at.óow* and its key role in many aspects of Tlingit culture.

29. Frederica de Laguna, *Under Mount Saint Elias: The History and Culture of the Yakutat Tlingit* (Washington, D.C.: Smithsonian Institution Press, 1972), 461.

30. Information in this paragraph is from Dauenhauer and Dauenhauer, *Haa Ḵusteeyí,* 219, 393 n. 4, and de Laguna, *Under Mount Saint Elias,* 827.

31. Dauenhauer and Dauenhauer, *Haa Shuká, Our Ancestors: Tlingit Oral Narratives* (Seattle: University of Washington Press; Juneau: Sealaska Heritage Foundation, 1999), 166–193; 194–217.

32. Harold Jacobs, "2003 Memorial Calendar," unpublished manuscript in author's possession, 2003, 2; David Katzeek, personal communication, May 2003.

33. Cheryl Shearar, *Understanding Northwest Coast Art: A Guide to Crests, Beings, and Symbols* (Seattle: University of Washington Press, 2000), 82.

34. Sergei Kan, *Symbolic Immortality: The Tlingit Potlatch of the Nineteenth Century* (Washington, D.C.: Smithsonian Institution Press, 1989), 182, 185.

35. Ibid., 185, 187. Cremation was the standard mortuary practice for all Tlingits except shamans. The deceased's ashes were put in a carved box and set on top of a mortuary pole within the boundaries of the village, often next to a house. The bodies of shamans, as beings who lived outside the cultural realm, were put outside the village in the forest, to return to the natural world with which they were associated.

36. Kan, *Symbolic Immortality,* 186; John R. Swanton, "Social Conditions, Beliefs, and Linguistic Relationship of the Tlingit Indians," in *Twenty-sixth Annual Report of the Bureau of American Ethnology for the Years 1904–1905* (Washington, D.C.: U.S. Government Printing Office, 1908), 441–442.

37. Kan, *Symbolic Immortality,* 183.

38. Ibid., 145.

39. Nora Marks Dauenhauer and Richard Dauenhauer, *Haa Tuwunáagu Yís, for Healing Our Spirit: Tlingit Oratory* (Seattle: University of Washington Press; Juneau: Sealaska Heritage Foundation, 1990), 47, 49.

40. Sergei Kan, "Memory Eternal: Russian Orthodoxy and the Tlingit Mortuary Complex," *Arctic Anthropology* 24, no. 1 (1987):52, 55.

41. Bill Holm, *Spirit and Ancestor: A Century of Northwest Coast Indian Art at the Burke Museum* (Seattle: Burke Museum and University of Washington Press, 1987), 154.

42. Kan, *Symbolic Immortality*, 185.

43. Rosita Worl, "Spiritual Food for the Dead: Tlingit Potlatch Bowls," *Alaska Native News* (May–June 1984):43.

44. Aurel Krause, *The Tlingit Indians,* translated by Erna Gunther (Seattle: University of Washington Press, 1956), 162.

45. Martha F. Betts, *The Subsistence Hooligan Fishery of the Chilkat and Chilkoot Rivers* (Juneau: Division of Subsistence, Alaska Department of Fish and Game, 1994), 14–17, 45.

46. Dauenhauer and Dauenhauer, *Haa Tuwunáagu Yís*, 125.

47. Rosita Worl, "The *Íxt'*: Tlingit Shamanism," in *Celebration 2000* (Juneau: Sealaska Heritage Foundation, 2000), 160.

48. Emmons, *The Tlingit Indians*, 370.

49. Worl, "The *Íxt'*," 165.

50. Anatolii Kamenskii, *Tlingit Indians of Alaska*, translated by Sergei Kan (Fairbanks: University of Alaska Press, 1990 [1906]), 86.

51. De Laguna, *Under Mount Saint Elias*, 683, 685.

52. Krause, *Tlingit Indians*, 202–203.

53. Martin H. Moynihan and Arcadio F. Rodaniche, "Communication, Crypsis, and Mimicry among Cephalopods," in *How Animals Communicate*, edited by Thomas A. Sebeok (Bloomington: Indiana University Press, 1977), 299.

54. Carol M. Eastman and Elizabeth A. Edwards, *Gyaehlingaay: Traditions, Tales, and Images of the Kaigani Haida* (Seattle: University of Washington Press, 1991), 35–39, 107–118.

55. Kan, *Symbolic Immortality*, 50.

56. John R. Swanton, *Tlingit Myths and Texts*, Bureau of American Ethnology Bulletin 39 (Washington, D.C.: U.S. Government Printing Office, 1909), 188–189.

57. Aldona Jonaitis, *Art of the Northern Tlingit* (Seattle: University of Washington Press, 1986), 92.

58. De Laguna, *Under Mount Saint Elias*, 677–678.

59. Kamenskii, *Tlingit Indians of Alaska*, 84.

60. Jonaitis, *Art of the Northern Tlingit*, 135.

61. Ibid., 136; Wilson Duff, "The World Is as Sharp as a Knife: Meaning in Northern Northwest Coast Art," in *The World Is as Sharp as a Knife*, edited by Donald N. Abbott (Victoria: British Columbia Provincial Museum, 1981), 216–217.

62. Swanton, *Tlingit Myths and Texts*, 82, 84.

63. Viola E. Garfield and Linn A. Forrest, *The Wolf and the Raven: Totem Poles of Southeastern Alaska* (Seattle: University of Washington Press 1996 [1948]), 73–77.

64. Marius Barbeau, *Totem Poles: According to Crests and Topics* (Gatineau, Quebec: Canadian Museum of Civilization, 1990 [1950]), 378.

65. Swanton, *Tlingit Myths and Texts*, 21.

66. See also Andrew Hope III, ed., *Traditional Tlingit Country (circa Late Nineteenth Century): Tlingit Tribes, Clans and Clan Houses* (Juneau, Alaska: Tlingit Readers, 2000).

67. De Laguna, *Under Mount Saint Elias,* 250–251.

68. Swanton, *Tlingit Myths and Texts,* 229–230.

69. Ibid., 3.

70. Dauenhauer and Dauenhauer, *Haa Tuwunáagu Yís,* 49.

71. Kan, "Memory Eternal."

72. Swanton, *Tlingit Myths and Texts,* 224.

73. Ibid., 165–169.

74. Ibid., 16.

75. Worl, "Tlingit *At.óow,*" 32, 70.

76. Garfield and Forrest, *The Wolf and the Raven,* 103, 105.

77. Nora Marks Dauenhauer and Richard Dauenhauer, *Haa Shuká, Our Ancestors: Tlingit Oral Narratives* (Seattle: University of Washington Press; Juneau: Sealaska Heritage Foundation, 1987), 219–243.

78. Swanton, *Tlingit Myths and Texts,* 6–7.

79. Garfield and Forrest, *The Wolf and the Raven,* 36–37.

80. Ronald L. Olson, "Social Structure and Social Life of the Tlingit," *Anthropological Records of the University of California* 26 (1967): 40.

81. De Laguna, *Under Mount Saint Elias,* 667, 197.

Suggested Reading

Boelscher, Marianne

1989   *The Curtain Within: Haida Social and Mythical Discourse*. Vancouver: University of
British Columbia Press.

The author draws from her field research in Masset, British Columbia, in the late
1970s to demonstrate the many functions of symbols and social roles in modern
Haida culture.

Dauenhauer, Nora Marks, and Richard Dauenhauer, eds.

1987   *Haa Shuká, Our Ancestors: Tlingit Oral Narratives.* Seattle: University of Washington
Press; Juneau: Sealaska Heritage Foundation. Reprint, 1999.

1990   *Haa Tuwunáagu Yís, for Healing Our Spirit: Tlingit Oratory*. Seattle: University of
Washington Press; Juneau: Sealaska Heritage Foundation.

1994   *Haa Kusteeyí, Our Culture: Tlingit Life Stories.* Seattle: University of Washington Press; Juneau: Sealaska Heritage Foundation.

The Dauenhauers' three volumes of Tlingit oral narratives, oratory, and life histories are presented in the Tlingit language with English translations on facing pages. The authors provide extensive notes and biographies of the storytellers and orators. Each volume includes a highly informative introduction and extensive information on Tlingit culture, history, and language.

de Laguna, Frederica
1972   *Under Mount Saint Elias: The History and Culture of the Yakutat Tlingit.* Three parts. Smithsonian Contributions to Anthropology 7. Washington, D.C.: Smithsonian Institution Press.

Although it focuses on Yakutat, this volume is widely regarded as one of the best general and in-depth descriptions of Tlingit culture and history. De Laguna, a leading authority on the Tlingits, recorded her field data between 1949 and 1954.

Emmons, George Thornton
1991   *The Tlingit Indians.* Edited with additions by Frederica de Laguna. Seattle: University of Washington Press.

Emmons, a U.S. Navy lieutenant in Alaska in the 1880s and 1890s, collected much valuable data and many Tlingit artifacts. De Laguna edited and added important commentary to Emmons's many notes and unpublished manuscripts.

Garfield, Viola E., and Linn A. Forrest
1948   *The Wolf and the Raven: Totem Poles of Southeastern Alaska.* Seattle: University of Washington Press. Reprint, 1996.

This book is a history and description of totem poles in three parks in Southeast Alaska. It describes the United States Forest Service program that restored and moved them from several small villages, the legends the poles display, and their role in Tlingit culture.

Holm, Bill

1983   *Box of Daylight: Northwest Coast Indian Art*. Seattle: Seattle Art Museum and University of Washington Press.

        Art historian Holm's detailed descriptions and extensive ethnographic commentaries supplement superb photographs of more than 200 pieces of Northwest Coast art.

Jonaitis, Aldona

1986   *Art of the Northern Tlingit*. Seattle: University of Washington Press; Vancouver: Douglas & McIntyre. First paperback edition, 1989.

        Jonaitis, a cultural anthropologist, compares secular and sacred Tlingit art through an analysis of the existing scholarly literature.

Kan, Sergei

1989   *Symbolic Immortality: The Tlingit Potlatch of the Nineteenth Century*. Washington, D.C.: Smithsonian Institution Press.

        Kan's years of fieldwork in southeastern Alaska and his use of previously unpublished Russian-language sources make this an invaluable resource for understanding Northwest Coast culture, especially its mortuary symbols and ceremonies.

Krause, Aurel

1956   *The Tlingit Indians*. Translated by Erna Gunther. Seattle: University of Washington Press.

        Based on information gathered during Krause's six months of work as a geologist in Alaska in 1881 and 1882, this volume is a unique and detailed account of Tlingit culture before it was changed by American and European contact.

Oberg, Kalervo

1973   *The Social Economy of the Tlingit Indians*. Seattle: University of Washington Press.

        Oberg, an anthropologist specializing in cultural economics, offers valuable insights into the economic aspects of Tlingit social structure and ceremonies such as the potlatch.

Stewart, Hilary

1993   *Looking at Totem Poles*. Seattle: University of Washington Press; Vancouver: Douglas & McIntyre.

Stewart's book is a useful illustrated field guide to more than 100 Tlingit and Haida poles at various outdoor locations in southeastern Alaska and British Columbia.

Worl, Rosita

2000   "The *Íxt'*: Tlingit Shamanism." In *Celebration 2000* (Juneau: Sealaska Heritage Foundation), pp. 159–172.

In this important article, Worl, a Tlingit scholar fluent in her native language, makes good use of late eighteenth- and early nineteenth-century Tlingit oral histories to provide a comprehensive description and analysis of Tlingit shamans and shamanism.